AN INTRODUCTION TO

CELTIC
MYTHOLOGY

DAVID BELLINGHAM

For he comes, the human child,
To the waters and the wild
With a faery, hand in hand,
From a world more full of weeping
than he can understand.

(William Yeats, *The Stolen Child*)

For Sheree and the Riders of the Sidhe

A QUANTUM BOOK

Published by Shooting Star Press, Inc.
230 Fifth Avenue, Suite 1212
New York, NY 10001
USA

ISBN 1-57335-313-2

This book was produced by
Quantum Books Ltd
6 Blundell Street
London N7 9BH

Creative Director: Peter Bridgewater
Designer: Sally McKay
Project Editor: Judith Simons
Editor: Henrietta Wilkinson
Picture Researcher: Ruth Sonntag
Illustrator: Lorraine Harrison

Typeset in Great Britain by
Central Southern Typesetters, Eastbourne
Manufactured in Hong Kong by
Regent Publishing Services Limited
Printed in Singapore by
Star Standard Industries (Pte) Ltd.

Contents

Introduction

OUR READING OF THE CELTS

Sad to remember, sick with years,
The swift innumerable spears,
The horsemen with their floating hair,
And bowls of barley, honey and wine,
Those merry couples dancing in tune,
And the white body that lay by mine;
But the tale, though words be lighter
    than air,
Must live to be old like the wandering
    moon.

(From *The Wanderings of Oisin* by William Yeats, 1889)

Yeats' lines provide a concise poetic summary of how aristocratic pagan Celts passed their days in hunting and fighting and their nights in feasting, dancing and love-making. It was during the feasting that the myths and legends of Celtic society were relayed by professional poets called bards; these early expressions of Celtic culture have not survived, for the simple reason that the bards relied on memory in the oral tradition. What was the subject matter and form of these early poems? The Roman writer Ammianus Marcellinus, writing in the fourth century AD, states that the Gallic Celts by that time had become civilized (he meant Romanized) but maintained their own Druidic religious philosophy and musical trad-

RIGHT **Uffington White Horse, Oxfordshire, England** *(chalk-carved figure; c. first century BC to first century AD?). There is no proven date for the carving of one of the largest pictorial works of art in the world. The taut curvilinear style, and location near an Iron-Age hill-fort, would suggest that the 111–metre (364-ft) figure was carved by the local Dobunni Celts to signify their territory. It may represent the Gaulish horse-goddess Epona as a patron deity of the Dobunni. The horse requires 'scouring' to keep it free of grass, an activity undertaken up to the last century by local people amid great festivity.*

itions: 'The bards celebrated the brave deeds of famous men in epic verse to the accompaniment of the sweet strains of the lyre.' Other sources as well as the later written versions of the myths themselves support Ammianus' statement, though 'epic' and 'lyre' were probably Graeco-Roman equivalents for whatever terms the Celts used. The original music and much of the epic poetry disappeared from the tradition when the myths were recorded by later Christian writers. However, some of the stories, dealing mainly with the heroic exploits of legendary Celtic warriors, have survived and make up the body of literature that we now call Celtic mythology.

Mythology can tell us many things about a society, ancient or modern. However, before we can begin to understand the nature of Celtic mythology, we must first of all deconstruct our own modern myth of the Celts. As can be seen from Yeats' early poems, during the late eighteenth and nineteenth centuries the main reference to Celtic myths was in Romantic texts: they provided a nostalgic escape from the Industrial Age back to an era ruled by 'nature' and 'magic' and peopled by heroic warriors and fair-skinned maidens. Each country's poets and painters rediscovered their own Celtic past: Ireland looked to pre-Christian legends such as the CuChulainn and Fianna (or Fenian) tales; Wales had the heroic saga of Pryderi in the *Mabinogion*; the Scottish poet James Macpherson (1736–96) forged his *Ossianic Ballads*, claiming them to be translations of a third-century Gaelic poet named Ossian; England resurrected the legends of King Arthur in works such as Tennyson's poem, *Idylls of the King*. The Romantic Age imbued the myths with their own romantic notions and often retained those elements of Christian medievalism which had become attached to the early written versions.

The Romantic vision of the 'Celtic Twilight' continues to influence our late twentieth-century perception of the Celts. We too require our dream-worlds and the word 'Celtic' conjures up mysterious moonlit landscapes with white-robed Druid priests performing strange rituals and brewing magic potions. Celtic art remains fashionable, particularly in jewellery: it has an abstract charm of its own and also signifies an attraction to an unknown past. Celtic literature weaves a similar spell: the narrator takes us from a world of seemingly real people and places into fantasy lands of fairies and monsters; his skill is such that we do not notice the transition. It is easy to be bewitched by such a culture.

We must ask whether the Celts themselves perceived their religion as a mystery and their poems as escapes from the real world. The answers are not readily forthcoming: the Celts did not write their own histories. Therefore, we have to learn about their customs and behaviour from the hands of contemporary Greek and Roman authors; although their view of the Celts was as mythical as ours, being based on the assumption that the Celts were uncivilized barbarians. Archeology has, however, confirmed some of the more extreme observations of the classical writers: the Celts do indeed appear to have performed human sacrifice and indulged in head-hunting. Archeology has also increased our knowledge of how the Celts lived, worshipped and buried their dead.

THE CELTS IN HISTORY

The earliest historical references to the Celts occur in Greek literature from around 500 BC. By this time they already appear to be inhabiting a wide geographical area, ranging from the upper reaches of the Danube in eastern Europe across to France and Spain. Archeological dating of Celtic finds

ABOVE **Gaulish stone with Celtic inscription** (Vieux-Poitiers, France; c. first century AD). The ancient Celtic language has not survived as literature. Our knowledge of it comes from place-names, names of tribes and kings on coins and inscriptions carved on altars or sacred stones. The letter-forms were borrowed mainly from the Latin of contemporary Romans; Greek letters were sometimes used in southern Gaul.

ABOVE **Irish cross-base inscribed with ogham and runic letters** (Killaloe Church, County Clare, Ireland; c. 1000 AD). The earliest Irish writings were in ogham script and date back to about the fourth century AD. Linear letters were carved on wood or stone across a central line and were differentiated by number and length of lines. Each letter was named after a tree or plant: for example 'd' was daur, meaning 'oak'. In Scandinavia, runic letters were used for the Teutonic (early Germanic) language. The oghams (right) read: 'A blessing upon Thorgrimr'; the runes (left) read: 'Thorgrimr carved this cross'.

THE CELTIC LANGUAGES

The pagan Celts spoke an Indo-European language which relates them in prehistory to the Greeks, Romans and Hindus. However, no record exists of the ancient languages, except brief inscriptions from the Roman period, and references in the classical authors to Celtic names. When the Celtic myths were finally written down in the early medieval period, the languages varied according to the author's country of origin: thus the Irish myths were recorded in Old Irish, but the contemporary Welsh form of the Celtic language would not have been understood by the Irish writers. It would appear that, by the time of the Roman invasion, any former cultural unity provided by a single Celtic language had disappeared: the Irish Celts were speaking 'Goidelic', while the British Celts were speaking 'Brythonic'. The Brythonic language seems to have been related to that spoken by the Gauls. Around the fifth century AD there were invasions and population movements in the western Celtic lands which led to linguistic changes: the Irish Goidelic language entered Scotland, later to become Scottish-Gaelic; the Anglo-Saxon 'English' language entered southern Britain, pushing the Brythonic language to Brittany.

THE SURVIVAL OF CELTIC MYTHOLOGY

Celtic myths were preserved in two main traditions: some were recorded by Christian writers and survive from the seventh century AD onwards while others have stayed alive in the oral folk traditions of Celtic areas. The apparent bias of the myths towards Britain and Ireland is due to the lack of surviving material from other former regions of the Celtic world, although surviving Celtic themes can often be observed in European folk-tales.

The earliest substantial survival of Irish mythology is a manuscript called the *Book of the Dun Cow*, containing versions from the CuChulainn sagas. Its Christian writer (author would be the incorrect term, implying an original creation) was a certain Maelmuri, whom historians know was murdered by Viking raiders in his cathedral at Clocmacnois in 1106. The curious title derives from a lost earlier manuscript of the seventh century AD written on cowhide (that of his pet cow!) by St Ciaran.

British mythology is now best known from the *Mabinogion* which was the title given by Lady Charlotte

ABOVE **Head of 'Medusa the Gorgon'** *(pediment of the Temple of Sulis Minerva, Bath, England; first century AD). The Greek female monster, with her snake-locks, was often used as an apotropaic figure in Greek and Roman religious contexts to 'avert the evil eye'. Here 'she' has become a 'he' complete with moustache and staring eyes in the Celtic style. Medusa's head was worn by Minerva on her breastplate to (literally!) petrify her enemies; her worship was combined with that of Sulis, the Celtic goddess of the healing waters of Bath. However, this 'Gorgon' has many unusual features, which may equally signify a Celtic sun deity, perhaps the consort of Sulis.*

Guest to her 1849 English translation of a collection of eleven Welsh tales preserved in earlier manuscripts: these are the *White Book of Rhydderch* of *c*1300–25 and the *Red Book of Hergest* of *c*1375–1425. *Mabinogi* means, broadly speaking, 'a tale of childhood': this was a mythical account of the conception, birth and early training of a Celtic hero. Lady Guest's word *Mabinogion* (which she incorrectly thought was the plural form) therefore implied that all eleven tales were of this genre. In fact only the first four 'Branches' are from an original *Mabinogi*; the other seven stories are of different genres and just happened to be included in the original manuscripts.

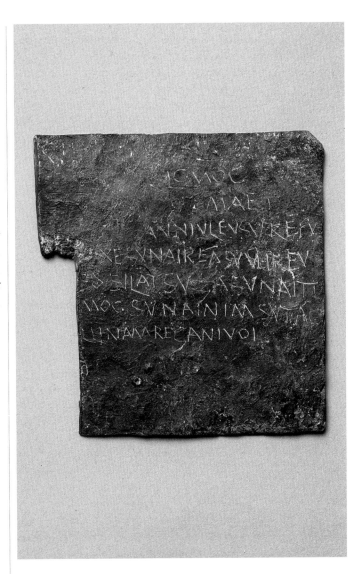

ABOVE **Pewter mask from culvert of Roman baths** (*Bath, England; first century AD*). *Many objects were thrown as offerings into the healing waters of Sulis Minerva. This may have been the face mask of a priest or priestess, held in front of the face during rituals.*

Celtic folk-tales survive in 'collected' versions recorded from the mouths of storytellers and singers by interested scholars. Unfortunately, with the advent of television in even the remotest areas of the Celtic world, the oral folk tradition is dying out. Although many of these folk-tales are simply good stories told by and for the rural community, there are some which preserve the 'high' myths and legends of the ancient Celtic ruling class.

THE NATURE OF CELTIC MYTHOLOGY

The bards were priests and teachers as well as entertainers and the behaviour of their mythical and legendary characters provided living Celts, both men and women, with ideals and thus ensured the continuity of the warrior society. Recurrent themes in Celtic mythology can therefore inform us about the preoccupations of their society. A love of beauty and bodily display is evident throughout the

ABOVE **Lead defixio (curse tablet) from Roman baths** (*Bath, England; first to second centuries AD*). *Curses were written in Latin onto lead strips which were rolled up and thrown into the spring waters; the curses invoke the goddess Sulis to bring harm to a personal enemy. Thus the Celtic goddess was believed to have harmful as well as healing powers.*

11

myths: when CuChulainn goes into battle, for example, his brightly coloured clothing, glowing jewellery and bristling hair are visual symbols of his heroic status. And heroines signify their own high and leisured status by wearing their hair in time-consuming intricate plaits, and by setting off their white unweathered skin with rich jewellery.

The world of nature was an unexplained and alien place to the Celts: therefore magical happenings tend to occur outside the stronghold, for example during the hunt; talking animals and birds feature in many of the stories; and Celtic divinities often represent the forces of nature. However, there is one important religious aspect which is often overlooked when we read the Celtic myths: scholars have demonstrated that the myths of other cultures tend to be narrative 'explanations' of historically attested religious rituals. Therefore, it is most likely that some of these stories were originally mythical explanations of religious mysteries or quests. So visits to the Otherworld might reflect an original rite of passage in which Celts passed from childhood to adulthood by means of a ritual period of absence outside the community. The Druidic philosophy encouraged a belief in immortality and the myths celebrate this idea: love persists beyond the grave in the form of intertwining trees on burial mounds; heads of dead heroes retain supernatural powers. Such beliefs were a consolation to the warrior society, where the hero's greatest glory was to die in battle.

Many elements in the surviving myths appear to mirror an earlier prehistoric 'heroic age' of Celtic culture, and thus the Celts of Caesar's day probably viewed their mythical ancestors with as much romantic nostalgia as did their admirers in the nineteenth century. However the myths also contain legendary representations of real historical characters, such as the fourth-century AD Roman emperor

Magnus Maximus who appears as Macsen Wledig in the *Mabinogion*. This historical example suggests that mythical figures such as Pwyll and Branwen, though unknown in history, might also have once existed in prehistory as real persons whose deeds were outstanding enough to have been preserved in both bardic poetry and folk memory.

The mythical world remained so integral a part of Celtic society that when Christianity arrived, the spoken myths could not be destroyed. Instead they were often Christianized or given Christian endings: gods became God; the Druid priests of the old religion were overcome by the Saints of the new religion. The greatest wonder of these stories is that they have survived for so many centuries and provide an enchanting window into the rich and varied past of the Celtic West. These myths are now ours, and we should read, feel and learn from them before handing them on to our children.

ABOVE **The Holy Well** *(William Orpen; tempera on canvas, 1916). The Irish symbolist artist has depicted the 'beehive' huts of a Late Celtic Arran community. The islanders are being converted to Christianity in the waters of their pagan well; Orpen's artist friend Sean Keating stands above the well, apparently unconvinced by the new religion. The deserted crofter's hut in the background and the shamefully naked 'Adam and Eve' in the centre reinforce Orpen's criticisms of cultural change in Celtic places.*

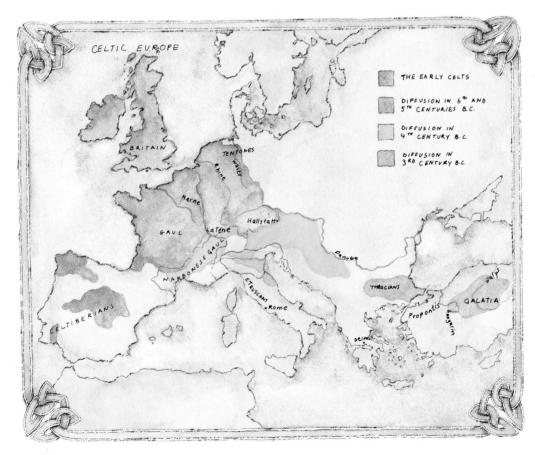

ONE

The Saga of CuChulainn

The pagan Iron-Age Celtic world of Ulster (ancient Ulaid) is graphically preserved, albeit as a mythological fantasy, in the Ulster cycle of early Irish storytelling. The young hero of the tales was CuChulainn, who bears some resemblance to the Welsh Pryderi: both births are associated with colts which the heroes later own, and both are renamed later in life. These stories served as an education for young Celtic noblemen, the vivid heroic characters providing them with models of youthful warrior behaviour. Details such as the miniature weapons and sports equipment reflect the military and athletic training of them The following extracts from the saga of CuChulainn are taken from the twelfth-century manuscript known as The Book of the Dun Cow, *the earliest surviving written version of the tales of CuChulainn and the Ulster heroes. Various themes and mythical features of the stories suggest early pagan origins, with the Celtic gods Lugh and Cu Rui appearing in human guise. As in the tale of the Welsh Pwyll, the storyteller presents his audience with an apparently 'real' ancient Celtic world of hill-forts and recognizable place-names. However, the 'fairy' world is never far away: 'real' landmarks such as New Grange burial mound (ancient Bruig na Boinde) exert their magical influence, heroes are born, and superhuman deeds are performed.*

The story begins with the appearance of strange birds wearing silver chains. Like the chains worn by the Children of Lir, these are tokens of their fairy nature, and the storyteller uses them to transport the warriors, and the audience, into the Otherworld.

THE BIRTH OF CUCHULAINN

In the days when Conchobar was King of Ulster, his chieftains noticed a flock of birds feeding on the grass of the plain by Emuin Machae, and they fed until they had laid bare the land as far as the eye could see. The warriors were bird-hunters and they set out in their chariots to pursue the birds wherever they might lead them. Dechtire drove the chariot of her brother Conchobar, and nine chariots sped across the plain after the birds. A silver chain linked each pair of birds and their flight and song was so beautiful as to enchant the Ulstermen.

Evening drew near and the Ulstermen searched for shelter for it was snowing. They were welcomed into a cottage by a man who gave them food and drink, and the Ulstermen were merry by nightfall. Their host announced that his wife was about to give birth and asked Dechtire to help. The Ulstermen brought in from the snow a pair of new–born foals and presented them to the baby boy whom Dechtire was nursing.

In the morning the Ulstermen woke to the sight of the boy and his colts, but the strange birds and the house had vanished; they were just east of the Bruig. Back to Emuin Machae they went, where the boy grew for several years until he suddenly fell ill and died. Dechtire cried from her heart for the death of her foster-son. She asked for water and a copper bowl was brought to her, but every time she raised it to her lips a little creature would spring at her mouth from the water, and every time she looked into the bowl, nothing could be seen. Dechtire's sleep was broken by a dream of the man in the phantom house. He told her that his name was Lugh son of Ethniu and that he had lured her to the house and that she was now bearing the seed of his son: the boy was to be named

Setanta and given the two colts which were meant for him alone.

When the Ulstermen saw that Dechtire was with child they wondered whether the father might be Conchobar himself, for brother and sister slept side by side. Conchobar saved his embarrassment by betrothing his sister to Sualtam son of Roech. However, Dechtire was mortified at having to sleep with her husband whilst already bearing another man's child, so one night she lay alone and crushed the baby in her womb. But Dechtire soon became pregnant again by Sualtam and a son was born.

RIGHT **CuChulainn,** *(John Duncan, 1866–1945). The Dundee artist drew on the style and medievalism of the Pre-Raphaelites to create his images of the Celtic heroes of literature and folklore. His pencil drawing portrays the Irish hero with tartan cloak and late Celtic brooch. The image is seen from the front, which reflects Duncan's love of Byzantine art, while the dreamy eyes point to the influence of Rossetti and Burne-Jones. Duncan's inscription applies to both hero and artist: 'I care not though I last but a day if my name and my fame are a power forever'.*

THE BOYHOOD EXPLOITS OF CUCHULAINN (SETANTA)

Conchobar had lost the allegiance of several Ulster chieftains after he had slain the sons of Usnach. These men had gone across to Connaught on the west of Ireland. One of them, Fergus, recounted the childhood of Cuchulainn to his hosts Ailill and Medb, King and Queen of Connaught:

'He was brought up at Mag Muirthemni in the south of Ulster. One day Sualtam and Dechtire told their son of the famous boys of Emuin Machae, whom Conchobar watches at play when he is not playing the board games or drinking his way to bed. CuChulainn asked Dechtire if he could go and see the boys. "You must wait until an Ulster warrior can go with you," she replied.

'"I want to go now," said CuChulainn. "Which road must I take?"

'"Go northwards," answered his mother, "but take great care, for the route is filled with dangers."

'"I shall go anyway," said CuChulainn, and he set off with his toy weapons, a tiny spear and shield; he also took his hurley stick and ball, hoping to play a game with the boys of Emuin Machae.

'At Emuin he walked straight out onto the playing field without first asking for the protection of the other players. The boys were angry at this lack of courtesy, for we all know the rules of behaviour on the playing field. They told him to get off the field and threw their three fifties of spears at him (for they numbered one hundred and fifty): every spear stuck in the tiny shield of CuChulainn. They hurled three times fifty balls at him and each one he held to his

RIGHT **Din Lligwy settlement, Anglesey.** *The entrance (right) of this late Iron-Age (fourth century AD) circular hut faces the central courtyard of a small Celtic settlement. It consisted of two circular and seven rectangular dwellings surrounded by a limestone wall; two of these contained evidence of iron smelting in their hearths. The roofs would have been of thatch.*

chest. They threw their three times fifty hurley sticks at him, but he caught them all.

'CuChulainn was furious: the hairs on his head stood on end and sparkled with his rage. One eye he closed to the size of the eye of a needle, the other he opened to the size of a bowl. He grimaced so that you could see down his throat and his teeth gleamed from ear to ear. The moon of the great young warrior rose from his head. I myself was playing chess with Conchobar when in ran nine of the boys with CuChulainn in hot pursuit. Fifty of them already lay outside where he had struck them down. "This is not sporting," shouted Conchobar.

'"They are the bad sports," answered CuChulainn, "for I wanted to join in their games, and they tried to throw me off the playing field."

'"What is your name?" asked Conchobar.

'"I am Setanta, son of Sualtam and your sister Dechtire."

'"Why," asked Conchobar, "did you not ask for the protection of the other players?"

'"I have not been taught the rules," replied CuChulainn.

'"Then will you take protection from your uncle?" asked Conchobar.

'"I will," said CuChulainn, "but one thing I ask of you, that I be allowed to undertake the protection of the three times fifty boys." Conchobar agreed, and they all went out to the playing field and the boys whom CuChulainn had knocked to the ground arose at the sight of their new hero.'

Conall, another of the Ulster chieftains, continued the story:

'We knew the boy when we lived in Ulster, and it was a joy to watch him growing up. Soon after the episode at the playing field related by Fergus, CuChulainn was involved in more heroic adventures.

'Culann the blacksmith invited Conchobar to a feast. Not too many were to accompany the King of Ulster, for the smith had only the wealth

LEFT **Head of the Romano-British deity Antenociticus, from his shrine at Benwell, near Newcastle-Upon-Tyne, England** (c. third century AD). *This local Celtic god was worshipped in a small temple near a Roman military fort on Hadrian's Wall. The shrine provides evidence of the adoption of native divinities by Roman soldiers. The head is carved in the classical manner, but its Celtic features shine through in the powerfully modelled eyes and hair.*

produced by his hands and his tongs. Therefore only fifty favourite old champions were to accompany Conchobar. Before they left Emuin, the king paid a visit to the playing field to bid the boys farewell; CuChulainn was single-handedly playing the three times fifty boys, and he was winning. When they tried to fill the goal with their balls, CuChulainn defended on his own and stopped every ball. Afterwards, in the wrestling, he threw them all to the ground; yet all three times fifty of them could not pin him down. In the game of stripping, he had the clothes off the lot of them, without even losing his brooch.

'Conchobar wondered at the feats of his nephew and he asked his men whether CuChulainn would grow into a man and perform similar heroic deeds: they all agreed that this would be so. "Come with us to the feast of Culann," said Conchobar.

'"I shall finish the games", replied CuChulainn, "and follow after you."

'At the feast, Culann the smith asked his royal guest whether all were present. "Yes," answered Conchobar, forgetting his foster-son, "and we are ready to eat and drink."

'"Well then," said the smith, "let us close the doors and make merry; my dog shall guard the cattle in the

fields: no man will escape him, for he requires three chains to hold him, and three men on each chain."

'Meanwhile, the boy was on his way to the feast, and to amuse himself he was throwing his ball in the air, and his hurley after it; and he was hurling his spear ahead and running to catch it before it hit the ground. As he entered the courtyard of Culann the smith, the dog went for him. The disturbance was heard by Conchobar and his men, and they watched from the windows as CuChulainn fought the dog with his bare hands. He held it by the throat and back and smashed it to pieces against a pillar. CuChulainn was taken into the house. "I am glad for your mother's sake," said Culann, "that you are alive. But that dog protected all my goods, and now I am done for."

'"Fear not," said CuChulainn; "I shall raise a puppy of similar pedigree for you, and until it is large enough to guard your property I myself shall be your watchdog."

'"Then we shall call you CuChulainn, 'The Hound of Culann', from now on," said Conall.

'Such were the exploits of a boy of six,' said Conall. 'What mighty deeds can we expect of him now that he is seventeen?'

THE FEAST OF BRICRIU

Bricriu 'Nemthenga' ('Poison-Tongue') invited Conchobar and the Ulstermen to a magnificent feast in a beautiful house designed specially for the occasion. Opposite the house Bricriu built a cottage with large glass windows so that he could see into the house, for he knew that the Ulstermen would not allow him to dine with them.

Before the feast Bricriu visited Loegaire, Conall Cernach and CuChulainn, three of the greatest heroes of Ulster, and told them of a prize which would be reserved at his feast for the champion of champions: 'You will become king of all Ireland,' Bricriu told each hero, 'if you win the champion's prize. You will receive a cauldron large enough to hold three warriors full of wine. You shall have a boar fed for seven years on milk and grain in the spring, curds and sweet milk in the summer, wheat and acorns in the autumn, and meat and soup in the winter. And you shall have a noble cow which for seven years has grazed on heather and milk, meadow-herbs and corn. And you shall have in addition one hundred large honey-cakes. This is the prize intended for you alone, for you alone are the greatest of the Ulstermen. You are to claim the prize as the feast begins.' So Bricriu tempted each hero and returned to finish the preparations for the feast.

The Ulstermen arrived on the day appointed for the feast, and each man and woman took their place in the great hall according to their rank. When all was ready the musicians began to play and Bricriu announced, 'Over there is the portion reserved for the champion. May the best man win.' And with those words he left the hall and entered his cottage.

As Bricriu had hoped an argument began immediately between Loegaire, Conall Cernach and CuChulainn, and soon the three warriors were fighting. Conchobar stepped between them and Senchae, who was the oldest and wisest of the Ulstermen, said, 'We should not have fighting during the feast. Tonight the portion shall be divided between all three of you, and tomorrow we shall ask Ailill, King of Connaught, to settle the dispute.' All agreed with these

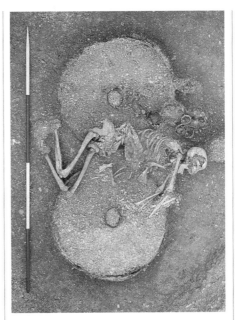

LEFT **Chariot-burial of young adult female, Wetwang, Yorkshire, England** (c. *second to first centuries* BC). *A square barrow marked the grave. The wheels and shaft can be seen alongside bronze female goods, including a mirror and work-box; a side of pork, often mentioned in mythology as 'the champion's joint', was included for the underworld meal. A similar male burial was found nearby, his Celtic warrior status signified by sword, spears and shield.*

BELOW LEFT **Handle of bronze bowl, Hallstatt, Austria** (*sixth century* BC). *An early example of Celtic metalwork. The myths abound with descriptions of such fine metal vessels at aristocratic banquets. The cow and calf are solid cast bronze and are depicted in a geometric style typical of Hallstatt art.*

words of wisdom and soon the company was merry with food and wine.

Meanwhile Bricriu was scheming in his cottage as to how he might set the great women of Ulster against one another. At that moment Fedelm, wife of Loegaire, came out of the house. 'Surely,' said Bricriu, 'you are wife of the greatest hero of Ireland. If you lead the women of Ulster back into the house tonight, you will forever be first lady of Ulster.' And Bricriu made the same promise to Lendabair, wife of Conall Cernach, and to Emer, wife of CuChulainn. The time came for the women to rejoin their husbands in the hall. They started walking at a stately pace, but as the house came in sight, they walked faster and faster until soon they were hitching up their dresses and running. The Ulstermen heard the commotion and, thinking that they were being attacked, barred the doors of the hall. The women hammered on them from the outside, as each wanted to become the first lady of Ulster. CuChulainn used his great strength to lift up a wall of the house and Emer was thus able to slip into the feast and claim her prize.

The feasting continued but soon the three heroes and their wives began squabbling once more over the

RIGHT **Gold amulets from Szarazd-Regoly, Hungary** (c. 100 BC). *These fine examples of miniature Celtic metalwork are formed from embossed gold-leaf with filigree and granulated decoration. The wheel symbolized the sun god and was used in burials as a protective talisman against the forces of darkness.*

champion's prize. It was decided that the three should journey in their chariots to either the King of Munster, Cu Roi, son of Daire, or to Ailill and Medb, King and Queen of Connaught: one of these would settle the dispute. They raced one another westwards across the hills and plains towards Connaught and Munster, and the ground shook beneath them.

Medb heard the commotion from the citadel at Cruachu and asked her daughter Findabair to go to the gatehouse tower of the fort and describe who was coming in such great fury: 'In the first chariot I see a man with long hair: he wears it in braids and from root to tip it changes colour from brown to blood red and golden yellow.'

'That is surely Loegaire,' said Medb, 'and he will slay all in Cruachu.'

'In the next chariot stands a man with the loveliest hair: like the manes of his horses is it braided, and his face glistens with red and white hues. He wears a blue and crimson cloak, and carries a shield with bronze edge and yellow boss; in the other hand he holds a spear of burning red, and the birds swoop around him.'

'That must be Conall Cernach,' said Medb, 'and he will cut us all to pieces.'

'And the third chariot,' continued Findabair, 'is pulled by the swiftest of horses: one is grey and one is black, and they run faster than the birds and they breathe flashes of lightning. And the warrior is a sad, dark man, the most beautiful man in Ireland; I see his white breast beneath his scarlet tunic, fastened with a golden brooch; his eyes gleam with jewels of dragon-red, and his brilliant red cheeks are aflame as he leaps like a salmon above his chariot.'

'That is CuChulainn,' cried Medb, 'and we shall be ground to dust by his rage.'

Medb welcomed the heroes with a vat of water to cool them off and fifty women to attend them in their guestrooms. They then told Ailill and

Medb that they had come to seek their judgement in the dispute over the prize of Bricriu; and all cursed Bricriu for his troublemaking.

Ailill could not make his mind up about the three contestants, so Medb took the judgement upon herself: 'There is no difficulty at all in judging them,' Medb told her husband, 'for Loegaire is as different from Conall Cernach as tawny bronze is from white gold, and Conall Cernach is as different from CuChulainn as white gold is from red gold.' She summoned Loegaire: 'I consider you to be king of all Ireland,' said Medb, 'and you are to have the champion's prize; you are to return to Conchobar and the Ulstermen and show them this as a token of our choice.' And she gave him a bronze cup, its base decorated with a bird in white gold, and Loegaire drained the wine in it, and joined his fifty women in bed.

Medb then summoned Conall Cernach, and said the same to him, and gave him a white gold cup with a golden bird on its base. He too drained the wine and went to bed; his fifty women were joined by Sadb Sulbair, daughter of Ailill and Medb.

Finally she summoned CuChulainn, and Ailill joined her in judgement. To the hero was given a cup of red gold, and the bird on its base was carved from a priceless gem. 'You are champion of champions,' said the King and Queen of Connaught, 'and your wife Emer is in our opinion the first lady of Ulster. Return to Conchobar tomorrow and claim the prize.' CuChulainn was joined in bed by Princess Findabair.

Before their departure on the next morning, the heroes entertained the court with their competitions. They played the game of throwing the wheel: Loegaire only managed to reach the top of the wall of the hall; Conall Cernach hit the ridge-beam to the cheers of the youth of Connaught; but CuChulainn's throw hit the ridge-beam so hard that the wheel flew out of the roof and landed an arm's length into the ground outside. CuChulainn then took the needles from the three times fifty women, and threw them one by one into the air, so that each was threaded in the eye of the next to form a chain. He returned each needle to its owner to the cheers of the crowd that had gathered in the courtyard. The three heroes then bade farewell to Ailill and Medb and the people of the fort of Cruachu and each returned separately to Ulster.

Conall Cernach and CuChulainn were held up by various adventures and when they eventually reached

LEFT **Human head on a large bronze cauldron from Rynkeby, Denmark** (*first century* BC). *He wears the warrior torc, and his stylized features are typical of Celtic representation. Heads of oxen also decorate this cauldron, and may have signified its use as a ritual container for animal sacrifice.*

21

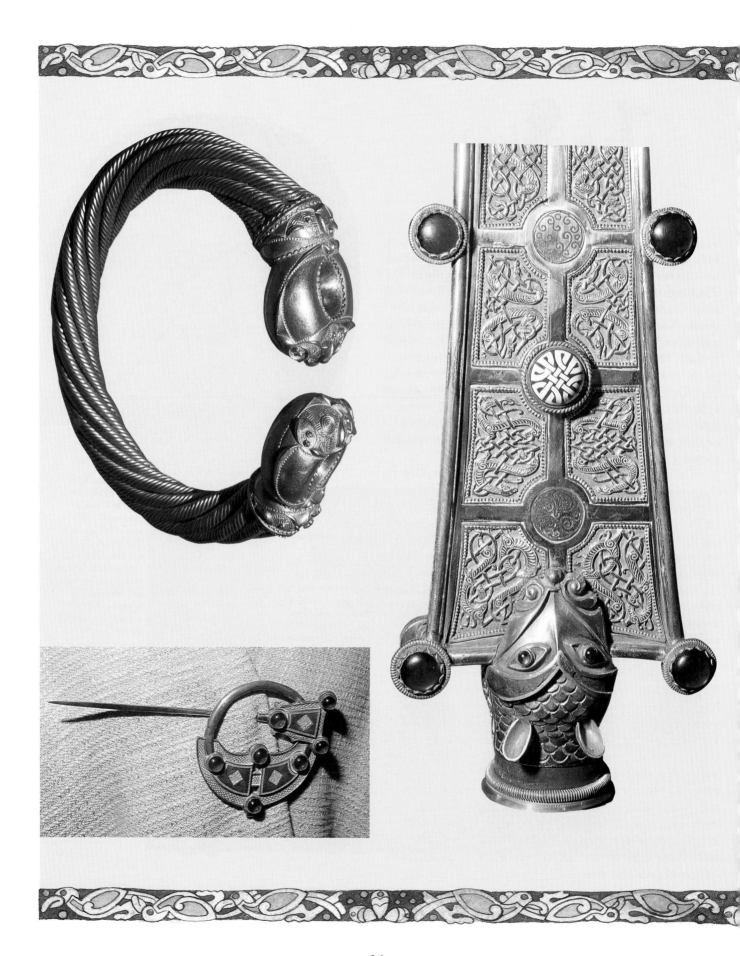

ABOVE LEFT **Electrum torc** (*from Snettisham, Norfolk, England; first century* BC). *Eight twisted wires make up each of the eight main strands; these were soldered onto the terminals, which were decorated with curving La Tène style ornaments. The British artists developed an increasingly insular version of the continental style.*

BELOW LEFT **Irish silver penannular brooch** (*seventh century* AD). *This type of brooch was exported from pre-Roman Celtic Britain to Ireland. By the early medieval period the Irish Celts were making their own extremely rich examples.*

LEFT **Base of the Cross of Cong** (*County Mayo, Ireland; bronze and oak; twelfth century*). *The Viking invaders influenced Late Celtic Irish art with its interweaving tendrils and dragons. The use of a beast to support the cross symbolizes the triumph of Christianity over 'nature'. The cross was made for the High King of Ireland, Turlough O Conna.*

RIGHT **Horse mask** (*from Stanwick, Yorkshire, England; first century* AD). *This bronze fitting was one of a number of horse trappings from the Celtic tribal centre of the Brigantes, destroyed by the invading Romans. The unnaturalistic features are typical of this period.*

LEFT **South door of the Church of St Mary and St David, Kilpeck, near Hereford, England** (*twelfth century*). *A rare example of Late Celtic art in medieval England. Interlacing tendrils, dragons and warriors decorate the columns. The door was restored in the nineteenth century with Celtic revival ironwork.*

The pagan Celts took their most treasured possessions into the grave and the finest examples of Celtic art appear in aristocratic tombs. Clothing accessories for both men and women, such as brooches, neck collars, torques and armlets, were of rich metals. Gold, silver or bronze were cast in flat moulds bearing Celtic designs or the metal was simply twisted and sometimes plaited to create more complex forms; some torques consisted of hollow tubes. Colour was provided by enamel inlays. Bronze hand-mirrors have been found mainly in women's graves, their backs incised with Celtic designs. Finely decorated metal horse-tackle, drinking bowls, swords, shields and helmets reflect the fighting and feasting of the myths and female as well as male chariot-burials provide evidence of the strong position of women in the Celtic warrior society. Celtic art also manifested itself in stone carvings connected with tombs and religious sites, but the most monumental expressions of the style are the huge figures carved into the chalk of downland hills: these have been interpreted as religious images or tribal emblems.

The work of Celtic craftsmen under Roman rule kept the artistic tradition alive: Celtic and Roman artistic styles can often be identified in the same art object. The Romans never penetrated Ireland and it is perhaps ironic that the 'golden age' of Celtic art occurred not under the patronage of pagan chieftains but within a Christian context. New metalworking techniques of filigree and granulation were learnt by the Irish artists in the seventh century AD. The old pagan interlaced designs now appeared on objects of Christian ritual – crosses, chalices and patens for Communion; reliquaries for the bones of saints; bishops' crooks as signs of the new spiritual leaders; and decorative letter-headings in Christian manuscripts. The richest Celtic brooches are also from this late period.

The most recent revivals of Celtic visual art occurred mainly in the works of late nineteenth-century Scottish painters such as John Duncan. They incorporated the old Celtic patterns into the clothing and furniture of scenes from the Celtic myths. These artists tended to romanticize the myths, according to the taste of their day. In the more recent Celtic revival, the artwork of the Devon painter Alan Lee has provided new romantic evocations of the ancient Celtic world in his book-illustrations of Welsh and Arthurian myths. Lee, like Duncan, has drawn on the decorative patterns of earlier Celtic artists to imbue his more realistic images with an authentic Celtic flavour.

LEFT **The Riders of the Sidhe** (*John Duncan; tempera on canvas, 1911). The Sidhe (Shee) ride out on Celtic Beltaine (May-Eve), to usher in the Summer. The Daoine Sidhe were the Irish version of British fairies, ancient heroes and deities who lived in the Sidhe or 'hollow hills' of the Otherworld. Duncan said that he could hear 'fairy music' as he painted. Duncan gives Celtic authenticity to his late Romantic images: horse-masks and trappings, and cup, sword and shield are all drawn from ancient examples.*

TWO

The Story of Deirdre of The Sorrows

This is one of the most popular stories in the oral tradition, and several versions of it were written down between the ninth and the nineteenth centuries. This is a slight adaptation of a version recorded from a Scottish Gaelic oral source in 1887, and is therefore in a 'folk' rather than a 'literary' style. The earlier Irish accounts gave Conchobar (Connachar) as Deirdre's father — presumably this relationship was considered too incestuous and altered in later versions — and the old prophet was Conchobar's Druid, Cathbad. The lovely Deirdre's Lament is from an early Irish account, and the story incorporates pagan divinities which would have been excized by Christianization. The names here are in their Scottish forms: Ferchar mac Ro, for example, would be Fergus mac Roigh in an Irish version.

In the early collections of Celtic literature, this is one of the Three Most Sorrowful Tales of Erin (which also include The Children of Lir and The Children of Turireann). It is an episode (probably an evening session in an elaborated oral recital) from a larger hero-tale and deals with the theme of the outcast. The detail of the intertwining lovers' trees may be compared to other love stories, including a version of Tristan and Isolt. A particularly Celtic feature is the powerful female characterization of the heroine Deirdre, including her wooing of the hero rather than waiting for his advances. Early cultural links between Scotland and Ireland are reflected in the story.

Malcolm Harper and his wife lived in a remote corner of Ireland; they wanted a child dearly. They had made offerings to the fertility goddesses but had little hope of success now that they were approaching old age. Unknown to them, however, their prayers were to be answered. An old man who could see what they could not see visited them with a message from the gods: 'You will have a daughter,' he promised, 'but she will be the cause of more bloodshed than this island has ever witnessed. Three men, all of them heroes, will lose their heads because of this woman, your daughter.'

By the end of the same year, a daughter was born but the mother was not even allowed a glimpse of her. Malcolm took the baby from the house and visited a childless woman who lived in their village. 'You can have the child,' said the father, 'but I want her out of this place, where no other living person will ever set eyes on her.' They travelled for three days until they reached the high mountains. On a mountain peak they dug a hole and covered it with a roof of mud and wood: here the foster-mother and baby girl made their home. Malcolm named his daughter Deirdre and departed.

The first sixteen years of Deirdre's life were spent in this humble bothy, which soon became part of the landscape, a green mound touching the blue sky. She saw no one but her foster-mother, who taught her everything that she knew about the flowers and birds which lived around them in the sunlight and the stars which visited them at night. Deirdre, unsullied by the greed and lusts of others, thus grew into a fair young woman. Indeed she was the fairest in Ireland, and if any man had looked into her face, she would have blushed fiery red. Her keeper, now an old woman, in obedience to Malcom made certain that this would never happen, leaving her in the bothy whenever she ventured into the valley for provisions.

In the white winters, kings and noblemen hunted wild boar and stag on the wooded slopes of the mountains. Deirdre would hear their screaming horns and feel the terror of the deer as it bellowed at the rising moon. Her keeper told her that these were the wild hunters of Cernunnos,

ABOVE **The mountainous Atlantic coast of Ireland.** *Landscape description was an essential skill for the Celtic bards: by locating the heroic activities of mythical characters within a recognizable world, myth became reality.*

31

RIGHT **Round tower at Clonmacnois monastic settlement, Ireland** (c. *tenth century* AD). *This Christian settlement was vulnerable to Viking boats sailing up the River Shannon: such defensive towers were typical of the early Celtic Christians in Ireland. It was here that the* Book of the Dun Cow, *a rich and early manuscript of Irish myths, was written on the hide of a pet cow.*

Allen and Arden had heard of Deirdre's beauty, and had in mind that their elder brother Naois might take her for his own wife: after all, she was as yet unmarried. It was dusk and they were hurrying to reach Connachar's court before nightfall. Deirdre, whose fleet foot was hindered by her courtly dress and shoes, called out after them in despair: 'Naois, son of Uisnech, how can you go without me?' The hero stopped in his tracks. 'What was that cry so harsh and yet so melodious?' 'It is the sound of the swans on Connachar's lakes. We must be near his castle,' replied the brothers. But Naois the hero recognized the voice of a woman in distress and turned to see Deirdre behind him. Deirdre, knowing her loved one to be the man who stood before her and forgetting her new courtly manners, stepped forward and placed three kisses on Naois' brow and one kiss each for Allen and Arden. Suddenly aware of what she was doing, Deirdre blushed a fiery red, but it was gone as quickly as the aspen quivers by the stream. To Naois she was fairer than the fairest vision.

Realizing the strife that this love would cause between himself and Connachar, his uncle's son, Naois took Deirdre on his shoulders and made his way out of Ulster. The three brothers took Deirdre across the sea to Alba, which some men call Scotland. They built a tower beside Loch Ness and were happy together hunting the deer of the mountain slopes and the salmon of the raging torrent.

The day finally arrived when Deirdre had pledged her hand in marriage to Connachar. The King of Ulster could not believe that the woman he loved so well would not return to honour her promise. She did not come. Connachar decided to avenge himself by taking her from Naois, whom he did not consider to be her rightful husband. Therefore he planned a splendid feast to which all the great kings and nobles of Erin would be invited; his uncle, Ferchar mac Ro, was sent off to Alba to give word of the feast to the sons of Uisnech; 'Tell them', said Connachar, 'that I shall not sleep again if they refuse my invitation.'

Ferchar mac Ro and his three sons sailed to Alba and soon reached the tower by Loch Ness. They were warmly welcomed by Naois who asked Ferchar for the news from Erin. 'A great feast is planned by the King of Ulster,' answered Ferchar, 'and the king has vowed by the forces of earth, heaven and the westward-travelling sun that he will not rest unless the sons of his father's brother Uisnech join the celebrations.'

'We accept Connachar's invitation,' said Naois.

Deirdre could see what the invitation really meant and tried to persuade Naois to remain in Alba. Knowing that words alone would not temper her husband's pride at being invited to such a feast of heroes, Deirdre broke into song:

'I had a dream, O Naois, son
   of Uisnech,
A dream for you to read.
On the warm south wind
   flew three white doves
Soaring over the sea,
Bearing in their beaks what
   every child loves,
Sweet nectar from the
   humble bee.

'I had a dream, O Naois, son
   of Uisnech,
A dream for you to read.
On the warm south wind
   flew three grey hawks
Soaring across the sea,
Bearing in their beaks three
   bloody torques
That meant the earth to me.'

And Naois sang:

'I read only the dreams of the
   fearful night,
In the morning they fade to
   dust, Deirdre,
In the morning they fade
   away.'

'And if we fail to accept the invitation from the great Irish king, we shall be an enemy to Erin forever,' added Naois.

Ferchar mac Ro was unaware of Connachar's grudge, and he pledged: 'If anyone should harm the sons of Uisnech, I, Ferchar, and my three heroic sons will fight to the death to defend you.'

Deirdre's sorrows began on the day they set sail for Erin: standing on the stern of the wooden ship she sang her farewell to Scotland:

'Across the waves I see you,
   Alba,
Slipping away from me,
I cry for your woods and quiet
   lakes
But my place is beside the
   one I love,
My heart is beside my Naois.'

And the sons of Ferchar sang:

'We weigh the anchor, hoist
   the sail,
And make towards the ocean
   deep,
In two days' time, come wind
   and gale,
Onto Erin's white shore we'll
   leap, we'll leap,
Onto Erin's white shore we
   shall leap.'

ABOVE **Celtic bronze torc from Dumfriesshire, Scotland** (c. *first century* AD). *Classical writers tell us that torcs were worn in battle by otherwise naked Celtic warriors. The taut abstract designs are found on many types of object in La Tène art.*

When they had arrived in Ireland, Ferchar sent a messenger to tell Connachar that the sons of Uisnech had accepted his invitation to the feast. Connachar was not ready for them, and asked them to wait for a day or two in a house reserved for important guests. That evening, wondering whether Deirdre was still the same fair girl that he had taken a year ago from the bothy, Connachar sent for Gelban Grednach, the Prince of Lochlin: 'Pay a visit to the sons of Uisnech, Gelban, and bring me word as to whether my Deirdre has the same fair skin as when she left Erin. If she has altered, then let the son of Uisnech keep her; but if she is still the woman of my dreams, then I shall have her back by the sword's point and the blade's edge.'

Gelban, known for his charm and cheerfulness, walked down to the house where the sons of Uisnech and Deirdre were lodging with the three sons of Ferchar mac Ro: Daring Drop, Hardy Holly and Fiallan the Fair were their names. He did not bother to knock at the door, but peeped at Deirdre through a hole in the door. Deirdre, conscious of the man's gaze, blushed a fiery red as was her wont. The effect was not lost on Naois who, realizing that a man must be staring at his wife through the peephole, picked up a dice from the gaming table and threw it hard at the small hole: his aim was sure, and cheerful Gelban the Charmer returned to Connachar minus an eye.

'You left the court charming and cheerful as ever, yet you return as cheerless Gelban the Charmless,' said the King of Ulster. 'Well, is my Deirdre as fair as when I last saw her?'

'I lost an eye through gazing at her in admiration,' replied Gelban, 'and would have remained to look at her with my other eye, but pulled myself away from the fair vision in order to report back to you.'

'Is she still so fair?' said Connachar. 'Three hundred of my bravest heroes shall take her from the house, killing those that are with her.'

into rocks with the poison of adders on their sharp edges. 'I am weary of this,' cried Arden, and the great-hearted Naois took his brother on his shoulders together with Deirdre. Arden was soon dead but Naois would not drop his brother in enemy territory. Allen was the next to fall and Naois took him on his back too. It was not long before he felt Allen's grip fail and, seeing both his brothers dead, Naois no longer cared if he lived or died: his heart burst as he sighed the bitter sigh of death.

'Success!' cried the Druid. 'I have destroyed the sons of Uisnech as you bid me, and you can now take your wife whom I have left unharmed.'

'Your education was worthwhile after all,' replied Connachar: 'Now clear the plain of your magic and let me see my Deirdre.' Duanan Gacha Druid did as he was told and the company of Ulster looked down on the plain. There they saw the three sons of Uisnech laid out on the green meadow side by side, and above them the bending figure of Deirdre, showering her loved ones with her tears and lamentations:

'O Naois, my most beautiful warrior, flower of all men; my lover who once stood so tall and powerful; my man of the shining blue eyes, dearly loved by his wife; I shall never forget the sound of your voice when we first met in the woods of Erin: as clear and true as spring water it was. From this moment I am unable to eat, drink or raise a smile to the world once so lovely. May my heart not break today, for the sea-tides of our everyday sorrows are strong, but I am sorrow itself, O Connachar.' And she looked towards the king who had brought this about.

The people of Ulster were watching and they asked their king what was to be done with the bodies of the three heroes. Connachar ordered that a burial pit should be dug and the brothers laid to rest beside one another. Deirdre remained there while the grave was being dug, encouraging the diggers to make the pit larger than was necessary. The sons of Uisnech were lowered into the grave and Deirdre sang her elegy:

'May Arden and Allen
   together lie,
As they stood together in life;
May Naois make room for his
   love Deirdre,
In death she remains his
   wife.'

Deirdre leapt into the grave as the salmon leaps in the raging torrent or as the deer bound on the mountain slopes; she placed herself beside Naois, son of Uisnech, and hand in hand they lay together in death. But Connachar's love for Deirdre also lay beyond death and he had her body lifted and buried on the opposite bank of the loch.

When the company departed into the twilight, a mountain fir sprouted from Deirdre's tomb and a second from the tomb of Naois; they grew towards one another, entwining themselves in a lover's knot above the still waters. They were cut down by the king, but they grew again.

BELOW **'Ossian's Grave': a neolithic grave above Glen Aan, County Antrim, Ireland** (c. 2500 BC). *The monumental stone graves of earlier cultures were revered as sacred by the Celts. The attribution of this grave to the Irish hero 'Ossian' (Oisin) was probably made under the influence of James Macpherson's spurious eighteenth-century Gaelic Romances of the Bard Ossian.*

RIGHT **The Children of Lir** *(bronze sculpture by Oisin Kelly, the Garden of Remembrance, Phoenix Park, Dublin; erected in 1966 to commemorate the 1916 Easter Rising). The sculptor has depicted the moment of metamorphosis from human to animal form as a visual mythological metaphor of political liberation.*

the previous night she had dreamt terrible things about her stepmother; but her fate was sealed, and into the chariot she went.

The five riders arrived at the Lake of the Oaks. 'I shall give you whatever you most desire in the world,' cried Oifa to the people dwelling there, if you kill the four children of Lir.' But the people would have nothing to do with her. Then she told the children to go for a swim in the lake and cast a spell upon them with a wand once given her by a Druid. And as she pointed the wand, she sang the spell over the waters and threw silver chains around the children's necks:

'Into the waters wild, royal
    offspring of Lir!
Forever more your cries will
    be lost among the birds.'

Immediately the four children began to sprout downy feathers and soon they had turned into beautiful swans of purest white. And Fingula sang:

'We know you for what you
    are, witch woman!
You have the power to make
    us swim the lake,
Yet we shall take our rest on
    land when we choose;
We shall be soothed, but you
    shall be scolded.
For though now you see us on
    the waves,
Our spirits are on their way
    home.'

'Lift the magic curse which you have laid upon us,' cried Fingula. 'Never!' Oifa laughed. 'Not until Lairgnen of Connaught marries Deoch of Munster, and southern woman is united with northern man. For nine hundred years you are to sail the lakes and rivers of Erin and no one will be able to lift my magic. One thing I grant you: the speech of man you are to keep, and no man or animal will prove equal to your poignant singing.' This last she granted out of sudden remorse; then she sang:

'So off with you now, young
    children of Lir,
From this time hence wild
    winds will mock you
Only to cease when Deoch
    and Lairgnen are wed,
And you swimming in the
    northwest of red Erin.

'My treacherous sword has
    pierced the heart of Lir,
Though in battle he be a
    great champion,
Yet the sword which enters
    him,
Is no victory to my wounded
    heart.'

Oifa rode on to the Hall of King Dearg. 'Where', asked the courtiers, 'are the children of Lir?'

'King Lir does not trust them in the Hall of Dearg,' she replied. Dearg was suspicious of Oifa, and sent messengers to the court of Lir to ask after the children. 'But are they not at the Hall of Dearg with Oifa?' asked Lir.

'No,' they replied, 'and Oifa told us that you were unwilling to let them stay with Dearg.'

Lir, troubled by the news, set off with his chariots for the Lake of the Red Eye, where his children were at that time. The swans heralded his approach and Fingula sang:

ABOVE **Silver torc from Trichtingen, Germany** (*c. second century* BC). *Decorated in a more linear, Eastern style, the bullhead terminals are symbols of the strength and virility of the Celtic warrior.*

43

'Our greetings to the
    company of horsemen
Drawing near to the Lake of
    the Red Eye,
Are these not men of magic
    and might
Seeking us out on the waves?

'Then make for the shore,
    brothers Aod,
Fiachra and beautiful Conn,
For these are no strange
    horsemen
But our father King Lir and
    his men.'

Lir heard the wonderful human voices of the swans and asked their names. 'We are the children of Lir,' they cried. 'Our stepmother has cast a cruel spell on us, as you can all see, and the spell cannot be lifted until the wedding of Lairgnen and Deoch.'

The swans sang their wild and woeful ballads, and Lir and his company wept and raged until the swans at last flew away. Thereupon Lir made his way to the Hall of Dearg and told him of his second wife's treachery. 'What creature', Dearg asked Oifa, 'would you least like to be in this world of shapes and forms?'

'Why,' she answered, 'anyone would hate to be transformed into a demon of the air.'

'Then become one,' said Dearg, and he pointed his own Druid's wand at Oifa. Immediately her face became demonic and her sharp wings took her away into the air to remain an air-demon until the end of time.

The children of Lir sang their songs of sadness to the clans who dwelt around the Lake of the Red Eye until they felt that the time had come to depart. Fingula sang to the people of Dearg and Lir as they stood on the shores of the lake:

'Fare thee well, Dearg our
    king,
You who have mastered the
    art of the Druids!
And fare thee well, dear
    father of ours,
King Lir of the Hill of the
    White Field!

'We are off to live out our
    final days
Far away from the dwellings
    of men.
We shall swim in the flowing
    tides of the Moyle,
Our feathers all bitter and
    salty.

'Till that day when Deoch
    joins Lairgnen,
Let us fly my brothers who
    once had red cheeks;
From the Lake of the Red Eye
    we travel;
In sorrow we fly from our
    loved ones.'

They flew away, high into the sky and out of sight, and took no rest until they reached the Moyle, the water which lies between Erin and Alba. And the people of Erin were so upset at the departure of the swan-children that a law was made banning the killing of swans.

The children found themselves cold and alone with a great storm brewing. Fingula suggested that they agree on a meeting place in case they lost one another in the tempest. 'Let us gather', said her brothers, 'at the Rock of the Seals.' And the lightning and thunder cracked at their words and the children of Lir were thrown apart on the raging deep. When at last it had died down Fingula sang:

'I wish I had died in the
    waters wild
For my wings have turned to
    ice.
My brothers three, come
    back again
And hide once more beneath
    my wings.
But I know that this can
    never be
Till dead men rise from their
    graves!'

She made her way to the Rock of the Seals and two of her brothers appeared, Conn and Fiachra, their feathers heavy with the salt thrown up by the stormy seas. Fingula cradled them under her wings: 'If only our brother Aod were here with us,' she

BELOW LEFT **Din Lligwy, Anglesey, Wales** (c. *fourth century* AD). *A well-preserved native British settlement from the late Roman period. The old Celtic cultural traditions survived in such remote areas, the circular and rectangular huts contrasting vividly with the contemporary luxurious Roman villas of southern England.*

cried, 'then we would be so happy.' Aod arrived with his head and feathers dry and preened. Fingula tucked him under her breast with Conn and Fiachra under each wing and she sang:

> 'The magical spells of a
>   wicked woman
> Have sent us into the
>   northern seas,
> Transformed by our
>   stepmother are we
> Into magical forms of swans.

> 'And now our bath is the
>   water's edge
> In the salty foam of the
>   breaking waves,
> And the only ale we drink at
>   the feast
> Is the salty draught of the
>   deep blue sea.'

One fine day a troop of gleaming white horses came galloping up and the swan-children recognized the two sons of Dearg. 'The king, our father,' they said, 'and indeed your own father Lir, are alive and well, but they have not been happy since you flew away from the Lake of the Red Eye.' Fingula then sang of their lot:

> 'There is meat and drink in
>   the court tonight,
> In the court of Lir is
>   rejoicing.
> But what has become of the
>   children of Lir?
> Our beds are our feathers,
> Our food is the white sand,
> Our wine is the deep blue sea.
> Beneath my feathers rest
>   Fiachra and Conn
> Under my wings they sail on
>   the Moyle,
> And beneath my breast lies
>   Aod dear,
> Together we lie in our feather
>   bed.

The sons of Dearg returned and told of what they had seen and the beautiful song that they had heard.

The flowing waters of the Moyle carried the children of Lir to the Bay of Erris where they remained until the fated day when they were to return to the Hill of the White Field. And there they found everything in a state of desolation; only nettles remained where once stood the high walls of dwellings. Three times they cried out their grief. Then Fingula sang:

> 'How sad it is for me to see
> My father's fallen halls:
> Here once were dogs and
>   hunting hounds,
> Here women laughed with
>   gallant knights,

> 'Here once was heard the
>   clash of cups
> Of horn and wood in merry
>   feasts,
> Now all I see is desolation
> My father long since dead
>   and gone.

> 'And we his children have
>   wandered for years,
> And felt the cruel blast of
>   freezing winds;
> But the harshest blow of all
>   has come:
> To return at last to an empty
>   home.'

The swans then flew to the lovely Isles of the West. At that time the prophecy of Fingula's song had come true: Deoch the Princess of Munster had promised to marry Lairgnen Prince of Connaught. But Deoch would not be wed until her prince had brought her the wonderful swans. Lairgnen found them swimming happily on the Lake of the Birds; he rowed out to them and removed their silver chains. In an instant they became human again, but the boys had aged into bony old men and young Fingula was now a bent and scrawny old woman. They died within the hour and were laid to rest as they had been in life: Fiachra and Conn on either side of Fingula, with Aod at her breast.

RIGHT **Bronze-Age grave on Shovel Down, Dartmoor, England** (c. 1000 BC). *The upland areas of western Britain provide the best surviving evidence of the Celtic landscape. Here there are Iron-Age farms and field boundaries, outside of which are the stone-circles and burial mounds of the preceding Bronze Age.*

Celtic Storytellers

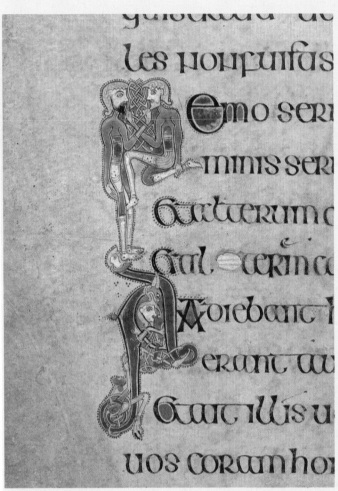

ABOVE **Beard-pullers and beasts from the Book of Kells** (*Irish; eighth to ninth centuries AD*). *The Christian scribes illustrated their texts with motifs and styles from the pagan Celtic past. The interlacing forms of human and animal figures symbolize the bestiality of man and nature in the eyes of the new religion.*

Our knowledge of the early pagan Celtic poets comes mainly from the recorded observations of their Greek and Roman contemporaries. Diodorus of Sicily, writing in the first century BC, tells us that among the Gallic Celts were 'lyric poets called bards, who accompany their songs with instruments similar to lyres: these songs include praise-poems and satires' (Book V, 31). This suggests that the bards played an important social role: they would be hired to write poems praising their patrons, but also to pour scorn on the patron's enemies.

The bards referred to by Diodorus did not record their poems in writing as did their classical counterparts, but passed them down from teacher to pupil in the manner of prehistoric Greek poetry. And like those early Greek poets, the bard was considered to be a kind of priest, passing religious mysteries on to future generations. This may account for the many 'unexplainable' aspects of the myths. Diodorus tells us in the same passage that they 'converse with few words and in riddles, mainly using obscure hints to refer to things and saying one word when they mean another; and they tend to use superlatives to boost their own achievements and put down those of others.'

The surviving Celtic myths themselves can also tell us about the status of the poets. In the story of the *Dream of Rhonabwy* in the *Mabinogion*, a poet sings a song of praise which can only be understood by other poets. In the medieval period there were highly paid and socially respected bards employed in the houses of the surviving Celtic nobility. There were also wandering minstrels who usually received small payments for their songs, but who certainly helped to keep the oral tradition alive by carrying the poems across Britain and Europe. It was in this period also that the first written versions of the myths were made, although since the scribes were usually monks, the stories were often heavily Christianized.

Finally there were the storytellers, who since time immemorial have told both heroic myths and folk-tales wherever there were people to listen, round the domestic hearth or in a corner of the pub. They still exist in the remoter Celtic areas and their feats of memory are legendary. A

fisherman in Barra is recorded as saying that when he was a boy he listened to the same storyteller every night for 15 years and that he hardly ever repeated a story.

The 'high' bardic tradition has survived in the annual Welsh Eisteddfod meetings, but there is also an attempt to revive it in less formal surroundings. The British singer and harpist Robin Williamson performs and records the Celtic hero-tales in spoken and sung poetry to the accompaniment of his 'Celtic' harp and the Breton artist Alan Stivell similarly recreates the Celtic myths of Britanny. The Celtic storytelling tradition is therefore still very much alive for those who wish to experience it.

ABOVE LEFT **Robin Williamson** *The Scottish songwriter and storyteller often accompanies his singing on the Welsh harp. A founder member of the Incredible String Band in the 1960s, more recently he has created sung and spoken versions of Celtic myths and legends. He has also written music and lyrics for a play of the* Mabinogion *and musical accompaniments for a television history of Wales.*

ABOVE RIGHT **A scribe writing a book** *(Anglo-Saxon ivory). Monastic scribes were the only literate men with the time and ability to record the oral Celtic myths in written form.*

FOUR

The Art of Description in Celtic Mythology

Celtic storytellers were experts in the vivid description of imaginary worlds, fantastic animals and superhuman characters. Bright colours and meticulous details of landscape, human appearance and dress are the main characteristics of Celtic descriptive passages, mirroring a similar manifestation of rich colour and detail found in the Celtic visual arts.

Descriptions of women tend to be highly voyeuristic and unrealistic, reflecting the male gender of the storyteller, and for the same reason, storytellers glamourized the warrior aspects of their male characters.

FANTASY LANDSCAPE: THE DISCOVERY OF PARADISE ON EARTH

The storm was over and the wind blew gently now; the sea-warriors hoisted their sail and the boat took in less water. A stillness fell upon the wide ocean, the waves were smoothed and it was bright and calm. Birds of different kinds never seen before filled the air round about with their singing. A land of graceful shape and fair shores came into view ahead of them; the sailors rejoiced at the sight of it. They sailed closer and entered a beautiful estuary, its green breasts hanging above silver-pebbled beaches, and in the clear waters the splendid deep purple of the handsome salmon flashed; and they looked about them and were pleased by the lovely streams running through woods tinged with purple.

Tadhg the Irish Prince of Munster stood at the bow and addressed his men: 'This is surely the island of our dreams, my fighting men; it is blessed with fruit and all things most lovely; we shall make for the beach, haul up the boat and give it time enough to dry out after its storm-battering.' Twenty stout warriors went on ahead with Tadhg, leaving twenty behind to guard the boat; and the wonder of it was that though they had come through wind and hard rain and the extremes of cold and hunger, they felt no desire for food and the camp fire

51

ABOVE **Bronze belt hook from the German Tyrol** (*fourth century* BC). *Early La Tène artists preferred running tendril patterns; here 'dragons' (or stylized horses, perhaps?) and human figures are depicted within such a fantasy pattern. Whatever the subject matter, it appears to symbolize the power of man (or god?) over beast, and would therefore have been fitting decoration for the aristocratic warrior.*

the men blink and look again, for they were white birds with purple heads and golden beaks. They sang the songs of minstrels as they ate their fill of the berries, and their music was plaintive and yet so soothing, that it would have lulled wounded warriors to sleep . . .

Anonymous Irish author of the fourteenth or fifteenth century

FANTASY WOMAN: A VISION OF ETAIN THE FAIRY

The men could see a woman beside the spring. In her hand glinted a comb of silver with decorative work in gold and she was about to wash her hair in a bowl of beaten silver with reddish-purple gems glittering on its rim and on its sides four inlaid golden birds could be seen as she turned the bowl. The woman wore the fleece of a fine shaggy sheep dyed purple, and on the shoulders of this cloak were silver brooches worked in twisted filigree with golden ornament. Beneath the cloak she wore, stiff yet smooth, a tunic of green silk with a long hood, embroidered with reddish-gold thread; they could see the interlacing of exotic animals worked into the tunic in gold and silver running over her breasts, shoulders and shoulder blades. The gold gleamed in the sunlight against its green silken background.

Her golden-blond hair was arranged in two long tresses; each tress was made up of four plaits, and at the end of each plait hung a bead. To some men her hair was the colour of the yellow flag iris which grows by summer water; others thought it like ruddy polished gold.

in that place. It was enough and more than enough to breathe in the incense of the trees, glowing with purple flowers about them.

Tadhg led them into the wood beside their path and they soon came to an orchard of glorious purple-fringed apple trees and oaks with leaves of lovely hue and hazels teeming with nuts of bright yellow. 'What a wonderful thing occurs to me,' said Tadhg to his warriors. 'It is winter back home, yet summer reigns here.'

There was indeed no end to the lovely places they discovered in that land. Leaving the orchard, they came upon a wood without shadows, with round purple berries the size of men's heads giving off wonderful scents; and the birds that fed on the berries made

52

flushed now with a purple as red as the blood of the frisky calf and now the white brilliance of snow. Her voice was noble and gentle; she walked as befits a queen, stepping steadily and stately. She was the most perfect woman in the world to behold, as fair and lovely as they could ever hope to see; the men agreed that she must have been a fairy . . .

Anonymous Irish author of the ninth century

ABOVE **Spring nymphs from the Roman fort at High Rochester, Northumberland, England** *(stone relief sculpture; third century AD). Many dedications to a Celtic water deity named Coventina have been found in northern England. This relief may portray a Roman goddess (Venus or Diana, disturbed while bathing) or it could also represent Coventina: classical iconography was often borrowed for Celtic deities. The original context is not known: it was reused in a water-tank at the fort.*

She began to untie her hair for washing, her arms reaching out from the openings in her dress. The arms were straight yet soft, their tops as white as a fall of night snow before the sun rises; the skin of her face was clear and her cheeks blushed red like the foxglove on the moor. Like the black beetle's wings were her eyebrows; like a spray of pearls were her teeth; like the brilliant blue starry flowers of borage were her eyes; of bright red vermilion were her lips. Her soft, smooth shoulders stood high and white; of the purest white were her fingers, long and slender as were her arms; and long, slender and soft as pliable wool were her white sides, like the foam on the wavecrest. Smooth, shiny and sleek were her warm white thighs; her small, firm knees were white and rounded; white shins she had, short and straight. She stood straight and even on her heels, which looked lovely from behind; if a straight rule were placed along her feet, no fault would be found, unless the skin or flesh were made to bulge by pressing too hard.

The bright blush of the rising moon glimmered in her noble face; her smooth forehead was high and dignified; the beams of eroticism shone from her royal eyes; her cheeks bore the dimples of her sport which

BELOW LEFT **Bronze armlet from Pitkelloney, Tayside, Scotland** *(c. first century BC). This massive piece of warrior ornament was originally polished and shining like all other Celtic bronze objects, with additional colour provided by red and yellow enamel inlay.*

FANTASY MEN: SOME HEROES FROM THE COURT OF KING ARTHUR

Morfran son of Tegid, was so ugly that he was thought to be an evil demon; therefore he was avoided in Arthur's last battle at Camlan. He was as hairy as a stag. Sandde Angel-Face was also left unharmed at that battle, but for a different reason: he was so beautiful that he was thought to be a heavenly angel.

There were three men, all sons of Erim, best known for their magical speed. Henbeddestr could run faster than any other man, even when they were on horseback; Henwas the Winged could run faster over even the shortest distance than any man or four-footed beast; and Scilti the Nimble-footed was often sent as a messenger by Arthur, for he would

ABOVE **Bronze helmet with decorated neck-guard** (*British; first century* AD). *The Celtic warrior's helmet was often highly decorated depending on his rank. This is a relatively restrained example with decoration in the taut curvilinear La Tène style: however, the holes on the crown might have held a plume or other fixture. Artistic representations of Celtic warriors depict them wearing animal crests, such as birds or boars; horned helmets were also worn.*

said to his wife, 'If there is anything of me in your son, my girl, he will be touched by a magic which removes the warmth from his heart and makes him headstrong. He will have other magical abilities: no one, from in front or behind him, will ever be able to see what he is carrying, however large or small it is; he, more than anyone, will be able to face fire and water; he will be the most loyal page and court official.

Then there was Gwallgoig, who used to keep whole towns awake with his bodily requirements when he was staying overnight: no one could sleep.

Osla of the Great Knife, who carried a short broad weapon at his side, used to be a boon to Arthur whenever he came to a torrent with his army. Osla's knife in its sheath would be placed across the narrowest point above the raging stream so that a bridge was formed broad enough to take the army of the three lands of Britain and its three offshore islands (England, Wales and Scotland, Anglesey, the Isle of Man and the Isle of Wight).

Gilla Stag-Legs was the champion of Ireland at long-jump: three hundred acres were his in one bound.

There were three more great heroes: Sol, who could stand on one foot for a day; Gwaddn Osol, who could level a mountain by standing upon it; and Gwaddn of the Bonfire, a boon to Arthur when his armies encountered woody obstacles: the sparks from his metal-studded soles were as large as pieces of red-hot iron drawn out of the forge.

There were the two great eaters, Hir Erwm and Hir Atrwm. On feasting days they would get their supplies by raiding three hundred towns. Then they would eat till noon and drink into the night; they would not stop eating in bed but would bite off the heads of the rats. When invited to another man's feast they would polish off the meat, be it lean or fat, hot or cold, sweet or sour, fresh or salted. Another eater was Huarwar, son of Halwn, who only smiled when he was

not bother with roads, but take the shortest route, touching the tree-tops and skipping the bog-rushes on the mountain slopes. Scilti was so light of foot that he never once bent or broke the rushes that he stepped on.

Teithi the Elder, son of Gwynham, who barely escaped when his lands were covered by the sea, had come to Arthur's court. Some magic curse was on his knife, so that no haft could be found to fit it; and therefore he lived a life of disease and misery, and died of it.

Drem the son of Dremidydd had eyes that could see the gnat in the rising sun's light as far away as Penn Blathon in Scotland from Cellig Wig in Cornwall.

Cynyr of the Beautiful Beard — some say that Cei was his son — once

LEFT **Horned warrior from Roman coastal fort, Maryport, Cumbria, England** *(Romano-British). This naïve and roughly incised image represents a naked horned warrior with shield and spear. His virility is symbolized by the horns and erect phallus: a straight-forward image of the male fighter ready for battle. Although crudely carved, the frontal staring face and wedge-shaped nose are in the high Celtic style.*

full. One of the Three Great Plagues of the West Country was caused by his demands to be given his fill from Arthur as a present.

There were a number of curious heroes. Sugn, son of Sugnedudd, had the ability to suck up the sea from beneath as many as three hundred ships, leaving only the dry sea-bed; he used to get red-hot heartburn. Cachamwri, one of Arthur's serving men, could work his way through a barn containing the crops of thirty ploughed fields: he would thresh around with his iron flail until the wooden posts, rafters and cross-beams were lying in as many bits on the floor as there were oats. When Gwefl son of Gwastad had the sulks, his lower lip would hang down to his navel and he would pull the upper lip over his head for a cap. The beard of Uchdryd Cross-Beard was so long that he had to throw its bristly red strands across the fifty rafters of Arthur's hall when he came to visit him.

FIVE

Pwyll, The Prince of Dyfed

The story of Pwyll is the first of the 'Four Branches' (or portions) of the Welsh Mabinogion collection and was probably first written down in the eleventh century. The Mabinogion deals with the birth and childhood of Pryderi, and this self-contained tale based on the hero Pwyll was probably once just the beginning of a complete saga dealing with the life and death of the hero Pryderi.

This relatively late, written version of the myth has lost little of its early pagan quality. The writer was not tempted to alter the powerful simplicity of his characters and reduce them to mythical 'types'. We are immediately plunged into a world where reality and myth intermingle: human characters with earthly passions encounter Otherworld and Underworld characters; one moment we are in a recognizable Welsh landscape, the next we are in a magical country. It is the Celtic storyteller's gift that he can take us in and out of these worlds without us noticing.

The mythological themes include the fathering of an earthly hero by a god; the false slandering of the hero's mother; and the linking of the hero's birth with the birth of a colt (as in the CuChulainn saga). The story is punctuated by hunting, banqueting and love-making, reflecting the preoccupations of the early Celtic chieftains for whom these wonderful tales were composed.

Pwyll ruled the seven cantrefs of Dyfed in the southwestern part of Wales, a land of high sea-cliffs and inland mountains. One day, while he was holding court at Arberth, he felt like going on a hunt in the woods of Glyn Cuch, where the hunting was good. When evening came he set out, stopping the night at Pen Llwyn Diarwya. Before dawn he was up and out with his dogs, loosing them at Glyn Cuch. Pwyll blew on his hunting horn and was off into the woods after his dogs; soon those that were with him were left far behind.

Pwyll followed the yelping of his hounds, but began to hear the cries of another pack mingling with his own. In a few moments he was at the edge of a clearing in the woods, and from the other side of the clearing a stag appeared, chased by the alien pack into the open ground. The hunter's gaze was diverted from the handsome stag to the dogs that brought it down: they were gleaming white in colour, with ears of glowing red. Pwyll entered the clearing and put the strange hounds to flight, so that his own might have their fill of the dead stag.

BELOW RIGHT **Cocidius as Silvanus, the Roman hunter deity** (*jasper seal-stone from Wall, near Hadrian's Wall, Northumberland, England; second to fourth centuries* AD). *Cocidius was a native Celtic hunter god, whose worship was taken up by Roman soldiers defending northern England. As no iconography existed for the Celtic god, the invaders depicted him as his Roman counterpart, the woodlander Silvanus: he is in hunting tunic with bow, quiver and hunting dog, and holds a captured hare; the tree may be the alder, sacred to the god. Silvanus/Cocidius signified the wild, uncultivated aspects of nature, and was therefore a fitting god for soldiers living so far from civilization.*

While all this was happening, the master of the strange hounds approached the clearing on a tall steed; and the horse was dapple-grey and the rider was in hunting clothes of similar hue, a horn hanging from his neck. He rode up to Pwyll and addressed him thus: 'Chieftain of Dyfed, I know who you are, but I refuse to offer my greetings.'

'Maybe your own rank', answered the prince, 'is such as to make that unnecessary.'

'My rank', the stranger answered, 'has nothing to do with it.'

'Chieftain,' said Pwyll, 'then where lies the problem?'

'May the gods hear me,' replied the horseman. 'It lies in your own lack of courtesy and breeding.'

'In what way have I been discourteous towards you, chieftain?'

'Why,' he answered, 'I have never met a man so impolite that he can bait his own hounds on a stag brought to the ground by another man's pack. That shows complete lack of courtesy, and, though I do not seek revenge, I shall make sure that you lose your honour to the tune of a hundred such stags.'

'Chieftain,' replied Pwyll, 'I have wronged you and will win back your favour.'

'How do you mean to do that?' asked the horseman.

'It depends on your rank,' said the prince. 'Tell me who you are.'

'I wear the king's crown in my own land.'

'My greetings then towards you,' said Pwyll, 'but what land is that?'

'My name is Arawn and I am King of the Underworld, which you mortals call Annwn.'

'My Lord,' cried Pwyll, 'then how shall I recover your good favour?'

'In this manner. Another king rules down in Annwn. His name is Hafgan and he makes repeated incursions on my territory. Get rid of him and you will win back my favour.'

'Tell me how,' said Pwyll, 'and I shall gladly do as you bid.'

'You will be joined to me by an oath of friendship,' explained the King of Annwn, 'and I shall disguise you as myself. You will rule in my place in the Underworld, and sleep with the fairest lady imaginable; and neither she nor others of my court will know that it is not me. We shall meet again at this trysting-place in a year and a day.'

'I agree to that,' said the prince, 'but how do I find King Hafgan?'

'One year from tonight,' answered the king, 'I have arranged a tryst with him at the ford yonder. You must come to that place looking like me, and you are to hit him with one fatal blow; and however much he entreats you to hit him again, hold yourself back, for if you hit him a second time he will be back fighting me again the next morning.'

'I agree to that,' said Pwyll, 'but what will become of my own kingdom of Dyfed?'

'I shall rule in your stead, and nobody will know the difference between us.'

'Well,' said Pwyll, 'I had better be on my way.'

'I shall be your guide, so that your path will be free of obstacles until we

reach my kingdom.' And Arawn and Pwyll descended into Annwn.

'This is my kingdom,' said Arawn, 'and my court is yonder. Go ahead now, all within will recognize you.'

Pwyll walked into the courtyard; on all sides were grand halls and sleeping-quarters; he entered the great hall and was surrrounded by squires who helped him off with his hunting boots. In came two knights who removed his hunting clothes and dressed him in a silken gown brocaded with gold. The hall was soon filled with a throng of handsome people: there were warriors with their pages, all fitted out with the finest armour; and there among them, dressed in a silken gown brocaded with gold was the fairest lady imaginable, the Queen of Annwn. The company washed their hands and sat at table, with the queen and the earl sitting on either side of the Prince of Dyfed.

Pwyll talked with the queen; she was of graceful temperament and the least affected and most eloquent of all the women he had ever spoken with. They wined and dined the evening

ABOVE **Teutonic gilt-bronze brooch from Denmark** (c. 500 AD). *The Teutonic tribes were probably originally close to the Celts of Eastern Europe; by the historical period (the time of the first written records) the two had become separate cultures. Similarities of style and subject matter can be seen in this brooch, with its decorative spirals, frontal wide-eyed faces and monster/human oppositions.*

away to the sounds of minstrels and drinking-songs. Pwyll had never in his life seen such a profusion of fine foods and drinks served in golden bejewelled cups and dishes.

When the time came for bed, Pwyll turned his back on the queen and remained silent until the morning, when they continued to speak with the gentle friendliness of the evening before; and however tender they were to one another by day, every night of the year was as cold as the first.

Pwyll filled this year with the hunt and the feast, enjoying the company and affection of his court, until at last the night arrived for his tryst with the rival king. That man had also remembered the appointment and as King Hafgan approached the ford of Glyn Cuch with his knights, a man on horseback stood on the opposite side of the river and addressed the company: 'Gentlemen, pay attention to what I say. This tryst is between the two men who claim the kingdom of Annwn as their own. The fight is for them alone, and you must stand watch.'

The two kings rode into the ford. Pwyll, King Arawn's substitute, was the first to strike: the blow fell on the central boss of Hafgan's shield which was shattered as was the king's armour behind it. Hafgan was fatally wounded by this single blow and was hanging the length of his arm and spear out of his horse's saddle. 'Chieftain,' he gasped, 'you have no right to kill me; I have not challenged you in any way, and I know no reason why you should wish for my death. But by the gods, now that you have mortally wounded me, put an end to me with a second blow.'

'Chieftain,' replied Pwyll, 'I may come to regret what I have done. You must find another to finish you: I will not do it.'

'Carry me away from this place,' said Hafgan to his knights, 'I can no longer be your king, for my death has at last been accomplished.'

'And gentle knights,' added he

who was acting on behalf of Arawn, 'take my advice and consider whether you are now my vassals.'

'Lord Arawn,' said the knights in unison, 'every man of us shall obey you as the sole king of Annwn.'

'Good,' replied Pwyll, 'I shall receive the submissive, and may the arrogant be humbled by the sword.'

The knights rendered homage to their new king and by noon of the following day the two old kingdoms of Annwn were in one man's power. It was now a year and a day since his first meeting with King Arawn and Pwyll made his way to the tryst at the clearing in Glyn Cuch. Arawn welcomed him: 'I have heard what you have done for me; may the gods reward you for keeping your oath of friendship.'

'Yes indeed,' said the prince, 'and when you return to your own land you will see the proof of what I have done in your name.'

'May the gods reward you,' said the king, 'for what you have accomplished on my behalf.'

ABOVE **Bronze shield-boss from the River Thames at Wandsworth, London, England** *(second to first centuries* BC*). The Celtic La Tène style is evident in this rich votive offering to the water gods by a warrior aristocrat: the taut curvilinear foliate patterns are imperceptibly combined with bird forms. The repoussé designs were hammered from behind the bronze plate; fine details were then engraved onto some of the resulting shapes to give them texture.*

61

RIGHT **Dragon Hill, Uffington, Oxfordshire, England.** *This distinctive hill lies close to the monumental chalk-cut White Horse on the side of the Ridgeway, an ancient track rich in prehistoric and Celtic remains and legends. A legend tells of Saint George killing the dragon on the summit: no grass can grow where its magic blood was spilled, hence the bare chalky patch. Saint George was originally a pagan smith god who also slew dragons: the new religion transformed him into a saintly Christian soldier.*

King Arawn returned the Prince of Dyfed to his proper appearance and took back his own from Pwyll. He rejoiced greatly on his way back to Annwn, for he had missed his warriors and court. They received him with the customary politeness since they were unaware of his absence. Yet the king spent the day in feasting and drinking, and spoke all day and evening to his wife and nobles. Weary of the day's feasting, at last they retired to their beds.

Arawn continued the evening's conversation in bed with his wife and, not having slept with her for a year, made love to her with great passion. She lay awake in the afterglow wondering at his sudden erotic fervour after a year of coldness. 'Why', asked her husband, 'have you gone quiet?'

'Why', she answered, 'do you ask me that after a year of quietness?'

'But', said he, 'we have always been close in bed.'

'I swear', said she, 'that for a year and a day we have neither spoken nor even faced one another in bed.'

That made Arawn think: 'By the gods,' he said to himself, 'my new comrade is an honourable man indeed.' And then he spoke the truth to his wife: 'My lady, do not blame me for what I am about to tell you.' And Arawn recounted his adventures in the Land of the Living. 'May the gods hear me,' said she, 'when I say that you have great influence over your friend for him to resist sensual pleasures and keep his faith.'

Meanwhile Pwyll had returned to his own lands in Dyfed and had made inquiries into what his subjects thought about his government over the past year. 'My lord,' they all replied, 'we have never known you to be so affable, lovable and generous.'

'By the gods,' he said, 'you should be thanking the man who really was with you. A year and a day ago . . .' And Pwyll told them his story. When he had finished his men said, 'Well, my lord, we have the gods to thank for such a friendship; but you will not grudge us the good that has been accomplished this year?'

'By the gods, of course not,' replied the Prince of Dyfed.

From that day onwards the two leaders continued to grow in friendship. They sent one another heartfelt gifts for the hunt: fine falcons, hounds and horses. Pwyll was greatly honoured by the people of Dyfed for what he had achieved during his year in Annwn; indeed, they considered that his bravery in uniting the two realms was such as to deserve a higher title than Prince of Dyfed: from that day onwards Pwyll, Chief of Annwn, was his name.

Some time later Pwyll was at his court at Arberth enjoying a great feast. After the first course, he felt like walking to the top of a mound, called Gorsedd Arberth, which towered up behind the court buildings. One of his courtiers warned him, 'It is said that if a man of noble birth takes his seat on top of the mound of Gorsedd Arberth, he will either come away covered with wounds, or else he will have seen something wonderful.'

'No one can harm me when I have so many of my men around me,' Pwyll replied, 'but I should like to see this wonderful thing.'

Pwyll and his men climbed the mound of Gorsedd Arberth, sat down, and waited. A lady appeared on the road beneath the mound. She rode a large pearly white steed, and was draped in silk brocaded with gold. The horse strode solemnly past the mound and Pwyll addressed his men: 'Do any of you recognize the rider?' None of them answered. 'Then one of you must go and ask her who she is.' One of the men ran down the mound, but at the roadside she had disappeared. He set off after her, but the

faster he ran the greater the distance between them. He gave up and returned to Pwyll: 'Lord Chief of Annwn,' said the man, 'it is pointless to follow her on foot.' 'Then,' replied Pwyll, 'take the swiftest horse from the stables and catch her up.'

The man galloped away but though his horse was fast and he used his spurs and whip, the lady receded from his view as before. The man returned to Pwyll: 'Lord,' he said, 'there is no faster horse in Dyfed. We waste our time in following after her.' 'Yes,' replied Pwyll, 'magic is the only explanation.'

On the following day they held another feast. After the first course Pwyll once again decided on a walk to the top of Gorsedd Arberth. A swift horse was taken with them. They had just taken their seats on the mound when the lady appeared once more, wearing the same dress and riding the

ABOVE **The goddess Epona on horseback.** *This Celtic deity was the patroness of horses. The Roman cavalry adopted her as their own protective goddess, and this sculpture is carved in a classical style. She may be linked with the mythical Rhiannon in the story of Pwyll: both are Underworld figures. In her right hand she holds what resembles a rose-garland, offered to her by worshippers.*

BELOW **Rhiannon**
(*watercolour by Alan
Lee; 1981). Alan Lee's
illustrations for the
Mabinogion combine
Celtic decorative
features with Romantic
medievalist images. A
pervading tone of dark
sepia produces a misty
'Dark Age' atmosphere
in the paintings, which is
broken only occasionally
by the unfading colours
of precious stone jewels,
metals or dyes. This
wonderful mixture of
styles is a perfect visual
counterpart to the
various cultural layers
imposed onto the myths
over the centuries.
Here, Rhiannon
appears as a medieval
Arthurian princess
looking back at her
pursuers. Her birds
were harbingers of the
Otherworld and their
singing at Harlech in the
tale of Branwen
suspends earthly time.*

same horse. 'Look there,' cried Pwyll, 'Yesterday's rider. Now one of you, take the horse and go after her!' The lady was just at the foot of the mound riding, as before, at a solemn pace; one of the men started off after her at a moderate canter. But still he could not catch her up, even though he broke into a gallop. Indeed the harder he drove his horse, the further she was from him. He gave up the chase and returned to Pwyll at the mound. 'Lord,' he said, 'you saw how hard I rode.' 'I saw,' answered Pwyll; 'there is no point in trying to catch her. But by the gods, there is some reason for her journey here, if only we could break her resolve to avoid us. Let us all return to the court.'

That night was spent in drinking and singing. On the following day after dinner Pwyll said, 'Everyone who was on the mound with me yesterday is to accompany me there once more.' And he told his stable-groom to saddle his horse and bring his spurs. Up Gorsedd Arberth they went and they sat down. The lady

came into view, in the same silken gold dress and on the same pearly white horse. After her rode Pwyll, but the faster he galloped the further she was from him. Soon he was riding as fast as he had ever ridden in his life, but he saw that he followed her in vain. So he called after her: 'Lady, for the sake of the man you most love, wait for me.'

'I am glad to do so,' she replied, 'and my horse wishes that you had made the request long ago.' She waited for Pwyll and, drawing aside her head-dress, fixed him with her eyes and spoke with him.

'Lady,' asked Pwyll, 'where are you coming from and going to?'

'I go my own way,' she answered, 'and I am pleased to meet you.' Pwyll thought that he had never seen a lady or maiden fairer than the one who was before him.

'Lady,' he asked, 'I would gladly know what you are doing in these parts.'

'Then I shall tell you,' she said; 'it is you I come to see. My name is Rhiannon daughter of Hefeydd the Elder, and he has pledged me in marriage to a man I despise. For my part I will marry no man save yourself. This is the reason for my journey here.' 'My answer to you, by the gods,' said Pwyll, 'is that there is no maiden or lady in the world that I would rather marry.' 'Then let us make a tryst,' she said. 'A year from now at the court of my father Hefeydd a feast shall be prepared for you.' 'I shall be there,' said Pwyll. They went their separate ways and Pwyll changed the subject whenever his men questioned him about her.

A year later Pwyll set off with a hundred men. They rode to Hefeydd's court and were given a great welcome. At dinner Pwyll sat at the top of the table, with Rhiannon and her father on either side of him. They had finished the meat and were beginning their drinking-songs, when a striking young man with reddish-blond hair entered the hall. 'The gods welcome to you,' called out Pwyll to the man,

64

for he looked of royal blood. 'Please be seated.' 'I shall not,' replied the man, 'unless you grant me what I am here for.' 'You shall have what you desire,' said Pwyll. 'Why did you give such an answer?' cried Rhiannon too late. 'He must keep his word,' said the stranger, 'in the presence of such nobles.' 'What is it you want, friend?' asked Pwyll. 'You are feasting,' he replied 'and shall sleep tonight with the lady I most love, and I am here to take your place.'

Pwyll was struck dumb by the stranger's words, and Rhiannon up-braided him for his stupidity: 'This is Gwawl son of Clud, the man who wishes to marry me against my will, and now you must let him have me or you will be dishonoured.' Pwyll did not know what to say. 'You must let him have me,' continued Rhiannon, 'and I shall make sure that he does not have me.'

'How can that be?' asked Pwyll in bewilderment.

'You can remain for the night's feasting, and I shall make a tryst with Gwawl: I shall promise to sleep with him in a year's time, but you are to come to the trysting place with a hundred knights. Leave them in the orchard by the court. Enter the hall in rags and ask him to fill this small bag with food: I shall put a spell on it so that it can never be filled up. When he asks whether it will ever be full, you must answer: 'Only if the greatest in the kingdom presses the food in with his feet.' And when he has his feet in the bag you are to pull it over his head and tie it; then you must blow your hunting-horn as a signal for your hundred riders to take the court.'

'Lord,' interruptd Gwawl, 'I am waiting for your answer.' 'You may take what is in my power to give,' said Pwyll. 'But these men of Dyfed,' added Rhiannon, 'are here as my guests, and they will enjoy the night's feasting. In one year's time I shall

66

prepare a feast for you, and then you may sleep with me.' Each chieftain returned to his own court.

When the year was up Gwawl son of Clud came for his feast at Hefeydd's court. Pwyll Chief of Annwn also came, dressed in beggar's clothing as Rhiannon had told him. At the height of the merrymaking, he entered the hall. 'May the gods be good to you and make you prosper,' called out Gwawl. 'The same to you sire,' replied Pwyll, 'and I should like to make a request.' 'So long as it is reasonable,' said Gwawl, 'you shall have what you ask.' 'Will you fill this small bag with food for me to keep the wolves from my door?' 'A humble request,' said he, and he called for the servants to fill the bag to the brim. They could not fill it and Gwawl asked: 'Will the bag ever be full?' 'Only', said Pwyll, 'if the greatest man in the kingdom presses the food in with his feet.' 'Go on then, my man

of valour,' said Rhiannon to Gwawl. And Gwawl had no sooner stepped into the bag than it was up over his head and its thongs were knotted. Pwyll shed his rags and blew his horn. The hundred knights who had hidden in the orchard were soon in the court; as each man entered the hall he smacked the bag and asked, 'What have we here?' 'A badger,' the others cried. And in this manner was first played the game of Badger in the Bag.

Inside the bag Gwawl protested: 'This is no honourable death for me, to be battered to death in a bag.' 'He is right,' added Hefeydd the Elder. 'I accept what you say,' said Pwyll, 'but what must I do with him?' 'This is what you must do,' said Rhiannon. 'The court poets and suitors are now at your command if Gwawl will make them over to you; and you must make him swear that he will not seek revenge for this night's events.' 'I swear,' called Gwawl, and he was let

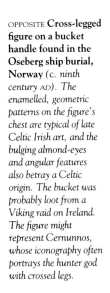

OPPOSITE **Cross-legged figure on a bucket handle found in the Oseberg ship burial, Norway** (c. ninth century AD). The enamelled, geometric patterns on the figure's chest are typical of late Celtic Irish art, and the bulging almond-eyes and angular features also betray a Celtic origin. The bucket was probably loot from a Viking raid on Ireland. The figure might represent Cernunnos, whose iconography often portrays the hunter god with crossed legs.

LEFT **Late Bronze-Age sacrificial well at Moen, Denmark** (c. 800–400 BC). The stylistic similarities in the art of non-Celtic northern Europe points to cultural connections during the Bronze Age. The well held votive bronze vessels and ornaments as well as animal sacrifices. There were also remains of joints of meat in an alder trunk.

RIGHT **The 'Monster of Noves', Bouches-du-Rhône, France** (c. *fourth century* BC). *Monsters devouring human bodies symbolized the triumph of death and the Otherworld over the Earth's living creatures. A victim's limb protrudes from this Gallic monster's jaws and his claws clasp severed heads, which were often taken in battle by Celtic warriors and used later for ritual purposes. The erect phallus symbolizes the Celtic religious connection between fertility and death, a theme which is present in the myths.*

out of the bag. 'Rhiannon has laid down the terms,' said Pwyll, 'and you must keep them.' 'All I want', said Gwawl, 'is to go home and take a bath for my bruises; my warriors can stay here as hostages.' And Gwawl limped away. The night was spent in food and drink, each seated as he had sat a year earlier. Later, Rhiannon and Pwyll went to their bed and enjoyed one another.

The next day Pwyll gave a feast for the court poets and suitors and all were content. At the end of the meal Pwyll addressed old Hefeydd: 'Lord, with your permission I should like to return to Dyfed tomorrow.' 'That is allowed,' said Hefeydd, 'but give Rhiannon good notice of when you would like her to follow you.' 'Lord,' answered Pwyll, 'I should like her to accompany me.' 'Is that so?' asked Hefeydd. 'Yes, by the gods,' said Pwyll, 'that is the way I shall have it.'

In the morning they set out for the court of Arberth in Dyfed. A warm welcome awaited them. A feast was prepared and all the most important lords and ladies in the kingdom were present. Pwyll sent each one off with a gift to remember him by: some took brooches, some rings, and some took jewels. Pwyll and Rhiannon brought prosperity to Dyfed over the next two years.

In the third year of their reign, the leading men of Dyfed summoned Pwyll to a place called Preseleu and counselled him to take another wife, since Rhiannon had not produced a child. Pwyll persuaded them to be patient for one more year.

Before the year was out, a baby was born to Rhiannon and Pwyll at the court of Arberth. Six women were called in to watch the boy's first night with Rhiannon; but by midnight they were all asleep, and when the cock crew they awoke to find the baby gone. 'What are we do to?' the women cried, 'for Rhiannon will blame us.' One of them answered: 'Look here, there is a hound in the corner with pups; let us kill the pups and scatter their bones in Rhiannon's

lap and smear her with the blood; all six of us will swear that she has killed her own baby.'

As the sun rose Rhiannon woke up and asked for her son. 'Lady,' replied the women, 'we tried to stop you, but see, you have battered your baby to death in the middle of the night.' 'You know that you are making this up,' answered Rhiannon, 'but I shall not harm you if you tell me the truth.' But the women kept to their story, and although Pwyll trusted Rhiannon's word, the Druids gave her a punishment: she was to sit outside the court by the horse-mounting block for seven years, and offer to carry in any man who would let her. Few allowed her to do this, but in this manner she spent most of that year.

In those days Teyrnon Twryf Liant ruled Gwent Is-Coed. He was the finest of men. He owned a mare more beautiful than any in the kingdom. Every year on the eve of May, the mare would foal, but no one had ever seen her colt. 'This May-eve,' said Teyrnon to his wife, 'I shall sit up and watch and find out who or what is taking our colts.' He had the mare brought into his room and in the middle of the night a colt was born: it was a handsome colt, large and already standing where it was born. Teyrnon was just remarking what a fine colt it was when all of a sudden there was a crash: a giant claw came through the window and grabbed the colt's mane. In a flash Teyrnon had drawn his sword and lopped off the monstrous arm at the elbow. There

BELOW **The 'Druid's Stone', Dartmoor, England.** *The hole in the rock was formed by the continuous action of running water over many centuries. A local legend refers to the stone as a place of Druid baptism: the initiate would be passed through the hole into the stream below. Many such legends survive as 'explanations' of natural and man-made curiosities in the landscape.*

69

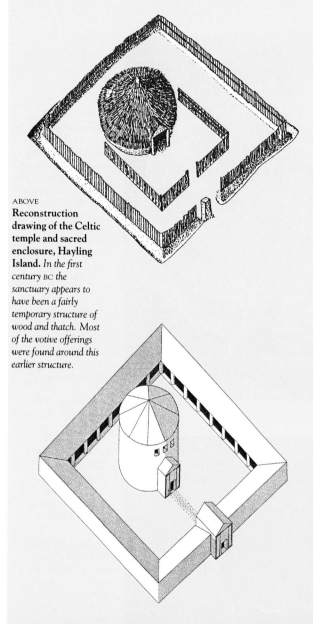

ABOVE
Reconstruction drawing of the Celtic temple and sacred enclosure, Hayling Island. *In the first century BC the sanctuary appears to have been a fairly temporary structure of wood and thatch. Most of the votive offerings were found around this earlier structure.*

into an inner circular gully with two larger post-holes at the entrance suggesting that the original building was a typical Celtic 'roundhouse' dwelling, probably roofed with thatch and with a doorway on its eastern side. However, excavations in the surrounding courtyard revealed the true function and approximate date of this early structure. The finds included votive offerings often grouped around burnt areas: sheep and pig bones; Celtic coins (dating the first building and subsequent ritual activity to around 50 BC onwards); horse equipment; and weapons.

All this material evidence suggested that the 'roundhouse' was actually a Celtic temple, typically orientated towards the rising sun, in use during the period of early Roman contact. Contemporary literary sources help to explain the wider context of the discoveries. Julius Caesar tells us (*Gallic War*, Book VI, 17) that the Celtic Gauls used to bring piles of booty from the battlefield to their sacred places, where they would dedicate them to a war god and accompany the ritual with animal sacrifice. Among the Hayling Island votive weapons were spearheads, intentionally bent during the rituals to signify the defeated enemy. The sanctuary was in a region of Celtic inter-tribal warfare until the Roman invasion, so there was ample opportunity for such military victory dedications.

Far from being destroyed after the Roman invasion in AD 43, this potent architectural symbol of Celtic religion was added to; a second building was put up by the Romans soon after the Claudian invasion. It was a larger and more permanent stone version of the Celtic temple, and apparently even more imposing. The width and depth of the surviving foundations suggest a high tower surrounded, like many other Romano-Celtic temples, by a covered portico. Roof tiles and eye-catching red wall-plaster were found which would have covered the temple's exterior, and an entrance porch had been built. There was no evidence to identify the deity, but a similar site in Gaul included an inscription to the Romano-Celtic war god, Mars Mullo.

It is interesting that there were far fewer votive offerings from the Roman period, suggesting that the site was now intended as a symbol of the dominant Romano-Celtic culture rather than as a place for native British religious ritual. This important evidence from Hayling Island not only confirms Celtic religious architecture and ritual, but also indicates the apparent continuation of Celtic religious activity during Roman domination.

Reconstruction drawing of the Romano-Celtic temple and sacred enclosure, Hayling Island. *After the Roman invasion of southern Britain in AD 43, the temple and sanctuary were rebuilt in more durable materials. The new buildings were larger and more impressive, but the ritual activities around the temple virtually ceased.*

Reconstructing Iron-Age huts at Butser Hill, Hampshire, England. *Archeology has provided evidence of sizes, shapes and materials used in building Celtic dwellings. The original Hayling Island temple probably looked like one of these roundhouses. Butser Ancient Farm has also launched experiments with Celtic farm animals, crops, cooking and pottery methods.*

LEFT **Temple of Vesunna (?), Perigueux, Dordogne, France** *(late first to third centuries AD). This rare survival of a Romano-Celtic temple gives some idea of the probable appearance of the second Hayling Island temple. The Gallic building was originally 24 metres (79 ft) high a....' (unlike Hayling Island) had an ambulatory: the holes for its roof beams can be seen 11 metres (36 ft) up. It too was orientated eastwards and had a larger galleried portico.*

SIX

The Story of Branwen, Daughter of Llŷr

This is the second of the 'Four Branches' of the Mabinogion. It hardly mentions Pryderi, and the oral tradition has evidently ousted the original 'childhood exploits' of Pryderi which would be expected in this part of his saga, and has replaced them with the exploits of the children of Llŷr. The Irish settings and mythical themes (the cauldron and the house built for Bendigeidfran for example) would suggest that an Irish storyteller intruded on the original Welsh saga of Pryderi at some stage of the oral tradition.

The grandfather of the children of Llŷr is named as Beli and probably refers to the god Belinus, a Celtic solar deity and legendary King of Britain. The mythological theme of the 'falsely slandered wife' (as with Rhiannon in the tale of Pwyll) recurs in this story. Here it is used as the trigger for revenge and war, reminding the reader of the Greek legend of Helen and the Trojan war. The 'iron-house' in which the giants are nearly killed reflects the pagan Celtic Iron-Age origin of the story, and while some scholars have suggested that it is a mythical version of human sacrifices practised by the Celts, others see it as the kiln used by the enamellers of Celtic jewellery. The Celtic religious notion of water as a supernatural dwelling is present here, seen in the lake from which the giants emerge.

RIGHT **The coast at Harlech, Wales.** *This west-facing stretch of the north-west coast of Wales provides the ideal setting for the tale of Branwen: shallow beaches provided landing-places for ancient ships, while the mountainous hinterland encouraged the building of strongholds, from prehistoric camps to medieval castles.*

The two sons of Llŷr, Bendigeidfran and Manawydan, were sitting on the rock of Harddlech (Harlech) which towers above the Irish Sea. Bendigeidfran was king of the Island of Britain and was staying at one of his courts at Harddlech in Ardudwy, on the north-west coast of Wales below the high mountains of Snowdonia. Beside them on the rock sat the two sons of Euroswydd, Nisien and Efnisien: the four men had the same mother, Penarddun, daughter of Beli, son of Mynogan. And when the sons of Llŷr were angry with one another, Nisien would be their peacemaker, but when they were on the best of terms, Efnisien would be sure to make trouble.

From the rock they saw thirteen ships come sailing from the south of Ireland; the wind was behind them and they approached the Welsh coast with great speed. 'Those ships', said King Bendigeidfran, 'are making for our shores. Let every man in the court arm himself and run down to discover their intentions.' The men went down to the beach and saw that the ships were finely fitted out with beautiful flags of brocaded silk. One of the ships moved ahead of the rest and they saw a shield held up above the deck with its point to the sky as a symbol of peaceful intent.

Small boats brought some of the strangers towards the rock where the king was seated. 'May the gods make you prosper,' he called from above. 'You are welcome. But tell me, who commands these ships?'

'My Lord,' they shouted back, 'they belong to the King of Ireland, Matholwch, and he is here with us.'

'Does he want to come ashore?' said Bendigeidfran.

'Not unless he succeeds in his mission,' answered the Irishmen.

'And what mission is that?' asked Bendigeidfran.

'My lord, our king would be your ally; he asks for the hand of your sister Branwen in marriage and thus to form a mighty union between Ireland and the Island of the Powerful.'

'Well, bring him ashore then,' said Bendigeidfran, 'and we shall discuss the matter.'

The Irish king and his men came ashore and made welcome that evening at the crowded court. The next morning Branwen was promised to Matholwch: she was one of the Three Matriarchs of the island, and the most beautiful woman in the world. It was decided that they should all journey to Aberffraw, Matholwch with his ships and Bendigeidfran by land; there the Irish king would sleep with the daughter of King Llŷr.

They all met at Aberffraw and entered a great tent for the feast, for Bendigeidfran was too large for any house. On either side of the King of the Island of the Powerful sat his brother Manawydan, son of Llŷr, and Matholwch; and next to the King of Ireland sat Branwen, the daughter of Llŷr. And when they had tired of talking, drinking and singing, they went to bed and Matholwch slept with Branwen.

Matholwch heard the news from his men. 'Your property', said one, 'has been harmed and harm will come to yourself.'

'But why', said Matholwch 'should they wish to do this to me when they have just given me such a lady of high rank and beauty?'

'Whatever the cause,' said another, 'the effects are plain to see. You must return to your ships.' And so the King of Ireland prepared to sail back to his own land.

ABOVE **The Gundestrup Cauldron, Denmark** (first century BC). On this silver inner panel of the gilt-silver ritual vessel, the artist depicted warriors going into battle, preceded by a ram-horned snake. The figures on the right blow carnyxes, or war-trumpets; some of the warriors have bird and boar crests, or horns, on their helmets; on the left, a god dips a human sacrifice into a bucket.

On the next day the men of Ireland were given billets for their horses and grooms on the land between the court and the sea. Efnisien, the troublemaking half-brother of Bendigeidfran, saw the billets and asked whom the horses belonged to. 'Why,' said the grooms, 'these are Matholwch, the King of Ireland's horses.'

'Will you tell me, then,' asked Efnisien, 'what they are doing here?'

'Why, our Irish king is on a visit to sleep with your sister Branwen, and the horses are his.'

'How dare they do such a thing to my sister without first asking me,' said Efnisien. 'I have never been so insulted in my whole life.' And he cut the horses' lips back to their teeth, their ears to their heads, their tails to their backs, and when he managed to catch hold of their eyelids he tore them from the bone. The horses were maimed beyond repair.

LEFT **Iberian bronze female figurine, from Aust-on-Severn, Gloucestershire, England** (c. fourth to third centuries BC). Similar objects are known to have been made in Spain. The glass-eyed figure was probably imported from Iberia along the trade-routes of the Atlantic coast.

When Bendigeidfran discovered that his royal guest was making ready to leave the court without giving polite notice, he sent messengers after him to question his motive. 'Is that not obvious?' replied Matholwch. 'I am amazed to have first been offered Branwen, the royal daughter of Llŷr who is, after all, one of the Three Matriarchs of the Island of Britain, and then to have received such outrageous insults as these.'

'No man in the court of Bendigeidfran committed this act, at least not with his authority.'

'I wish I might believe you,' said Matholwch, 'but the insult stands.'

The messengers reported Matholwch's words to Bendigeidfran. 'We must not allow him to leave in anger,' said the king. 'Brother Manawydan, take messengers and offer him the finest replacements for his injured horses; take him also this silver staff and golden plate and tell him that I know that my half-brother committed this crime, and that it would be difficult to punish him with death. Let him come and discuss peace on his own terms.'

Matholwch and his men accepted the offer and that night another great feast was prepared in a tent as before. Bendigeidfran noticed the change of heart in his new ally and decided to improve his peace-offerings: 'You are to have a cauldron of magical strength: for if one of your men is killed, and you throw him into the cauldron that evening, by the morning he will have revived to perfect health except that he will have lost the power of speech.' And Matholwch was exceedingly pleased with the new gift.

The next day Matholwch received new horses from the surrounding territories and once more they sat together at dinner. 'Tell me,' said Matholwch, 'how did this cauldron come into your possession?'

'Well,' replied Bendigeidfran, 'it was brought to me from Ireland by Llasar Llaes Gyfnewid and his wife Cymidei Cymeinfoll. You must know

the story of how they fled from the white-hot House of Iron, for this escapade took place in your own island.'

'Yes, lord,' said Matholwch, 'and I can complete it for you. One day I was out hunting on a mound which overlooks the Lake of the Cauldron. I saw a reddish-blond man emerging from the lake carrying a cauldron; he was huge and monstrous and was accompanied by a woman twice the

size of him. They came towards me and I greeted them. The man addressed me, saying, "This woman is going to conceive a son at the end of a month and a fortnight, and the son will be born fully armed and ready for battle." I took the pair of them into my care. For a year they behaved themselves, but the following year they began to cause disturbances in the land, molesting both ladies and gentlemen. Soon everyone hated them and a petition was raised for me to destroy the pair. This was not easy because both of them were so huge and strong. Therefore blacksmiths came from all over Ireland and built an iron house. The monstrous pair were tempted in with plenty of food and drink. And when they were drunk a great fire was lit around the house of iron, but they escaped through the wall with a mighty shoulder-charge. Presumably they then came across the sea to you with the cauldron?'

ABOVE **The Gundestrup Cauldron, Denmark** (*first century* BC). *This interior silver panel represents a divinity and warrior grappling with a wheel. The wheel is a solar symbol in Celtic art, and it is interesting that griffins are also depicted as these were Greek monsters associated with the sun-god Apollo. The Celtic god could be any one of a number of sky divinities.*

79

BELOW **Gilt-silver brooch from Ardagh, County Limerick, Ireland** *(c. eighth century AD). The meticulous golden filigree and granular decoration of this late Celtic penannular brooch would have signified a high degree of wealth and social status in the wearer.*

'No,' said Bendigeidfran, 'I shall tell you how the cauldron came to me. I allowed the pair to go where they please on my island, for wherever they went they built grand fortresses for my warriors.'

It was a feast of great joyfulness, and the kings talked well into the night. The following day Matholwch set out with Branwen for Ireland; they sailed from Aber Menei in their thirteen ships. There was much rejoicing in Ireland at their return, and every noble man and lady who visited the king brought Branwen some lovely brooch or ring or perhaps a royal jewel from their own treasure. Branwen was a favourite with everyone, and that year she bore a son who was named Gwern, son of Matholwch. He was sent away for a fine education.

But as it became known how Matholwch had been insulted during his visit to Wales, there was a change of spirit in Ireland. Soon even those close to him were demanding revenge and Branwen was forcibly put in the kitchens to cook for the court, and to have her ears boxed daily by the butcher when he had finished with the meat. 'And you must refuse permission', added his men, 'to any ship wishing to travel to Wales. And likewise you must take prisoner any who come from there.'

Meanwhile, Branwen trained a starling and taught it to speak so that it might talk of the insults she was suffering in Ireland. She tied a letter under its wings and sent it off across the sea to her home, where at last it found Bendigeidfran at his court of Caer Seint in Arfon. It landed on his shoulder and spread its wings so that all might see the letter. They realized that the bird was tame and the letter was read aloud to the court. When Bendigeidfran learnt of his sister Branwen's unhappiness he gathered a great army from the whole island and they decided to make war on Ireland. Seven lords were left behind at Edeirnon to guard the realm, and for this reason the town became known as Seith Marchawg ('Seven Riders'). The chief of them was Cradawg, son of Brân.

Bendigeidfran set off with the gathered armies of Britain and he himself waded across the sea, for in those times the water was deep but not wide. On the hills above the coast of Ireland the swineherds saw a marvellous sight and came to tell Matholwch: 'We have seen marvels today,' they said, 'for across the sea we have seen a forest and beside it a mountain, where there was neither forest nor mountain before; and what is more, they are moving towards Ireland.'

Matholwch was baffled by the report and sent messengers to ask Branwen if she could explain the phenomenon. 'I am no lady as you call me,' she replied, 'but I know what this marvel is. The forest is a fleet of ships and the mountain is my brother Bendigeidfran, for he will come by wading as there is no ship big enough to hold him.'

'But,' said the men, 'we also saw a ridge on the mountain with two lakes on either side.'

'My brother's angry eyes on either side of his nose,' laughed Branwen.

Matholwch called on all the armies of Ireland to come and take counsel, and they decided to retreat across the River Llinon (Shannon or Liffey) and break down its bridge, for the river was full of rocks which would obstruct the British boats.

ABOVE **Branwen** (*watercolour by Alan Lee; 1981*). *Branwen sends her starling to Wales bearing the message of her dishonour at the hands of the Irish. On the frame, Alan Lee has depicted the Welsh fleet sailing across the Irish Sea; the eyes and arms of Bendigeidfran can be seen above and to the sides of the main painting.*

geidfran and his men and the other half is for yourself and all of us.'

Bendigeidfran accepted the offer on Branwen's advice. The house was indeed built, but the men of Ireland had planned a trick. On all the pillars of the house they fixed pegs, and from every peg was hung a sack, and in every sack they hid an armed warrior. Efnisien entered the house and immediately questioned one of the Irish as to the contents of the bags: 'What is in this one?' he asked and squeezed it hard. 'Only flour, friend,' answered the Irishman. Efnisien asked the same question and received the same answer of all two hundred bags; he squeezed one so hard that the man inside was crushed to death.

The men of both islands entered the hall and Gwern, son of Branwen, was invested as the new king. He greeted Bendigeidfran and Manawy-

Bendigeidfran and his fleet arrived at the river. 'How can we cross over this river?' asked his men. 'There is no bridge,' answered Bendigeidfran, 'so I as your chief shall be a bridge for you.' (That was the first saying of this well-known proverb.) He lay across the river and the armies passed across him.

The Irish armies sent messengers to offer the kingdom of Ireland to Branwen's boy Gwern, son of Matholwch: 'This is to repair the wrong that Matholwch has committed to you and your sister,' said the messengers. 'It is up to you to decide what will become of Matholwch.'

'I am rather inclined to become King of Ireland myself,' answered Bendigeidfran, 'unless you come up with better terms than that.'

The messengers returned to Matholwch and told him to think of a better offer. 'What do you all suggest?' said Matholwch.

'Well,' they replied, 'he has never been able to find a house large enough to hold his great body. So we suggest that you have such a house built, and that half of it should contain Bendi-

ABOVE **Clapper bridge over the Waller Brook, Dartmoor, England.** *These primitive bridges are believed to date back to the Saxon period. The area is rich in Bronze- and Iron-Age settlements and the Celts would also have had to cross these streams; their bridges were probably of wood.*

dan, the sons of Llŷr; Nisien, son of Euroswydd called him over, and the boy went as a willing friend. But he would not approach Efnisien. 'Why does the boy avoid me?' said Efnisien; 'after all, I am his uncle.' Bendigeidfran sent him across to Efnisien, who cried: 'May the gods witness the atrocity I am about to commit.' And he took hold of the new boy king and threw him head-first into the great fire. When she saw her dying son, Branwen in her despair tried to jump into the fire with him, but her brother Bendigeidfran held her back, protecting her with his shield in the fight that followed.

Many warriors died that night. The Irish took the magic cauldron and built a fire beneath it, casting their dead into it until it was full: the next morning they would be as good as new, save that their power of speech would be gone forever. Efnisien realized that the cauldron was not for the dead of the Island of the Mighty: 'May the gods hear me in my distress,' he cried, 'for I have led so many of my countrymen to their deaths. I shall win back my honour and redeem the Island of the Mighty from defeat.' He lay down unseen among the Irish dead and was thrown into the cauldron by two survivors.

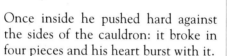

Once inside he pushed hard against the sides of the cauldron: it broke in four pieces and his heart burst with it.

Efnisien's deed brought but small assistance to the Island of the Mighty. Bendigeidfran's foot had been wounded by a poisoned spear and only seven of his men survived: these were Manawydan; Pryderi; Glifieu, son of Taran; Taliesin; Ynawg; Gruddieu, son of Muriel; and Heilyn, son of Gwyn the Old.

Bendigeidfran ordered his men to cut off his head: 'Take it to the White Mount in London,' he said, 'and bury it there facing France. Your journey will take some time. Rest at Harddlech for seven years of feasting; the birds of Rhiannon will sing to you and my head shall be as good company as it was when it sat on my shoulders. Your next resting place will be for eighty years at Gwales in Penfro. The sign for departure will be the opening of the door which looks across Aber Henfelen towards Cornwall; from that moment you must not rest until my head is buried in London. Now cross the sea to Wales.'

His head was cut off and the seven crossed over to the other side, Branwen and the head of Bendigeidfran with them. They landed at Aber Alaw in Talebolion. Branwen looked back across the sea to Ireland and at her own Island of the Mighty. 'Pity that I was ever born,' she cried, 'for I am the cause of the destruction of these two fine islands!' She sighed to the heavens and her heart was broken. She was buried by her companions in a four-sided tomb on the banks of the River Alaw.

The seven men carried the head to Harddlech. On the road they met a group of travellers. 'Any news?' asked Manawydan.

'None,' they replied, 'except that Caswallawn, son of Beli, has conquered the Island of the Mighty and now wears the crown in London.'

'Then what has happened to the seven men we left behind as guardians under the leadership of Cradawg, son of Brân?'

'Six of the men were killed by a sword without an owner: Caswallawn held the sword, but wore a magic cloak to make him invisible. Caswallawn would not kill his nephew Cradawg, but his heart was broken by what he saw. Cradawg became one of the 'three men whose hearts were broken by despair'. One young man, Pendaran Dyfed, fled into the woods.'

They reached Harddlech where they feasted for seven years. While they were eating and drinking, three birds sang them a song lovelier than any they had ever heard; and though the birds hovered far out to sea, their song was clear within the hall.

After seven years they made for Gwales in Penfro, where they were entertained in a fine royal castle which towered above the sea. The hall had three doors, two of which stood open. 'We must not open the third door,' said Manawydan, 'for it looks towards Cornwall.' The eighty

LEFT **Bull-headed terminal of iron firedog, Capel Garmon, Denbigh, Wales** (c. *first century* BC). *One of a pair used to support roasting spits over a fire, the bull was a Celtic symbol of virility and would have been a fitting decoration at a warrior banquet.*

RIGHT **Wooden figure from Ralagan, County Cavan, Ireland** (c. *first century* BC). *Before they learnt stone-carving techniques from the Greeks and Romans, the Celts used carved wooden images as representations of deities and/or worshippers. This male figure originally had an attached phallus and may have been a fertility god.*

years were spent without cares in joyful feasting, for they did not age and the head of Bendigeidfran was as cheerful as it had been in life. This feasting was called the Gathering of the Wondrous Head. The earlier feasting in Ireland was called the Gathering of Branwen and Matholwch.

One day, when the eighty years were up, Heilyn, son of Gwyn opened the third door and the company looked out across Aber Henfelen towards Cornwall. The memory of the loved ones lost in battles came flooding back and they mourned the loss of their chief Bendigeidfran. From that moment they did not rest until the head was safely buried on the White Mount of London. That deed was one of the Three Happy Hidings, although one day it would become one of the Three Unhappy Findings, for no plague could cross the sea until the head was found.

This ends the adventures of the men who travelled from Ireland, but those who stayed in Ireland fared worse. No one survived the battle except five women who were hidden in a cave deep in the wild countryside. Each woman carried a son inside her, and when those five sons were born, they grew into fine youths with a desire for marriage. Each son married one of the five mothers, and the land was divided into five and ruled by each. This is how the five provinces of Ireland came into being. They returned to the sites of the earlier battles and found plenty of gold and silver, enough to make them very rich.

Here ends this branch of the *Mabinogion*: we have heard of the insult to Branwen, one of the Three Unhappy Blows on the Island of the Mighty; and of the Gathering of Bendigeidfran, when the armies of one hundred and fifty-four districts crossed the sea to Ireland to avenge the insult to Branwen; we have heard of the seven years feasting at Harddlech and the songbirds of Rhiannon; and we have heard of the eighty-year Gathering of the Wondrous Head.

The Arthurian Legends

In general, the kings, queens and heroes of the Celtic myths are not otherwise known in history, although exceptions occur in the Welsh *Mabinogion*. Cassivellaunus, for example, appears in history as the Belgic chieftain who led the defence of Celtic Britain during Julius Caesar's second Roman invasion in 54 BC: in myth he becomes Caswallawn, the King of Britain, in the tale of *Branwen*. The tendency for myth to ignore the historical realities of time and space can be seen in the placing of Caswallawn in London, which was founded over 100 years after Cassivellaunus fought Caesar. Such inconsistencies between fact and fiction are unavoidable when real men and women become legendary heroes and heroines, and nowhere is this more apparent than in the Arthurian legends.

The earliest mythical tales of King Arthur and his court to appear were probably written in Welsh in the tenth century: the story of *Culhwch and Olwen* is certainly one of the first. In that story we are presented with a pagan Celtic world with quite different social codes to the later Arthurian legends. The poems of the twelfth-century writer Chrétien de Troyes provide the earliest versions of Arthurian romance – the polished medieval conventions of courtly love are epitomized in Lancelot's love for Queen Guinevere; brash warriors of Celtic tradition are transformed into handsome knights; and heroic quests for elusive Druidic tokens become Christian pilgrimages in search of the Holy Grail. Many other medieval Arthurian romances followed and the tales of King Arthur and his Knights of the Round Table were soon well known throughout Europe. Gradually, these loosely connected stories were bound together into 'complete' versions as the quests of various knights were woven around the central heroic figure of Arthur himself, and what were originally non-Arthurian romances, such as *Tristan and Isolt*, were also incorporated.

The late medieval popularity of the Arthurian legends is demonstrated by the fact that Sir Thomas Malory's prose version, *Le Morte d'Arthur* (1485), was one of the earliest

84

LEFT **Merlin as a stag** (*medieval manuscript; Bodleian Library, Oxford, England). Merlin had the Celtic sage's ability to shapeshift. The transformation into a stag is in the pagan tradition of horned warriors and gods such as Cernunnos: the stag signified powerful animal strength.*

RIGHT **King Arthur riding a goat** (*mosaic from Otranto Cathedral, Italy; twelfth century). The British hero is found in medieval art from all over Europe. Here he is identified in Latin as 'Rex Arturus' in a southern Italian mosaic which incorporates both biblical and pagan figures.*

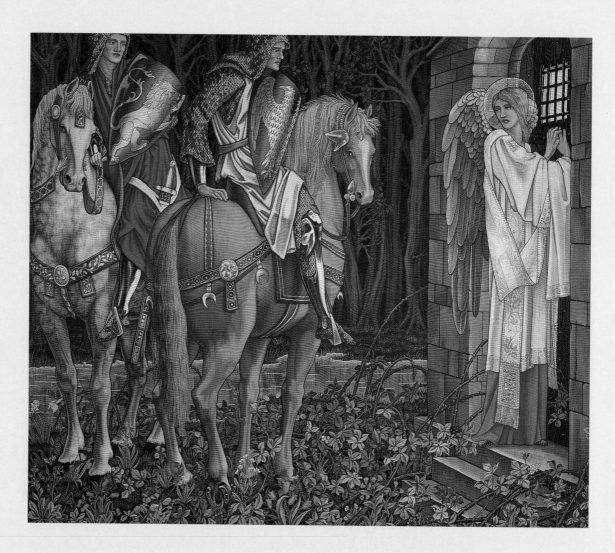

printed works in English. The mythical Arthur fell from favour during the seventeenth century and the Age of Reason, however, but late eighteenth- and nineteenth-century Romantic writers of both prose and poetry revived the medieval Arthurian romances, culminating in the Victorian period with Lord Alfred Tennyson's poem, *Idylls of the King*. The music world also explored the romances; the German composer Wagner found large audiences for his Romantic Arthurian operas *Lohengrin*, *Parsifal* and *Tristan and Isolde*. The twentieth century has kept the tradition alive in music, film, art and literature with novels by TH White, Rosemary Sutcliffe, Mary Stewart and Alan

Garner being just a few of the many works which have dealt with the Arthurian legends, directly or indirectly.

The 'real' historical Arthur has been almost entirely transformed by the romantic legends of the medieval and modern periods. Early accounts of the man, as found in the ninth-century *History of the Britons* and the twelfth-century Geoffrey of Monmouth's *History of the Kings of Britain*, are dubious since their historical 'facts' are extremely questionable. However, cautious use of these sources together with the mythical 'evidence' point to a famous Celtic Romano-British warrior, fighting for a Britain left defenceless by the departure of the Roman legions in the early fifth century. Arthur's enemies probably included the Celtic Picts and Scots, but his major battles would seem to have been against the non-Celtic Anglo-Saxons. The mythical hero-worship in court poetry and folklore of such a patriotic figurehead would have been compounded by the lack of contemporary written literature.

Geoffrey of Monmouth's 'mythical history' began in earnest the tradition of associating episodes from the Arthurian legend with real topographical locations. The most famous of these is Tintagel Castle in Cornwall, which since medieval times has been referred to as the legendary birthplace of Arthur. The highly dramatic setting must have inspired early medieval romantic interpretations, and in return the legendary associations with ancient kings would have encouraged the building of the thirteenth-century castle by the earls of Cornwall. More recently, 'Merlin's Cave' at Tintagel was named after the Arthurian magician for the benefit of late nineteenth-century tourism, and a Victorian lead-mining tunnel became 'King Arthur's Mine'.

Until recently, Tintagel 'island' was believed to have been a monastery, lacking any signs of possible Arthurian connections. But a fire in the 1980s revealed further features and finds which showed it to have been an important community in the late Roman period. More excitingly from the Arthurian point of view, the site appears to have developed into a powerful post-Roman stronghold and centre of trade in the fifth and sixth centuries. However, a separate medieval folk tradition presented Tintagel as the palace of the legendary King Mark of Cornwall with its Tristan and Isolt associations. Such is the power of myth and legend to impose itself on landscapes.

ABOVE **The Four Queens Find Lancelot Sleeping** (*Frank Cadogan Cowper* [1877–1958]; *oil on canvas, 1954*). *Cowper was one of the last British painters to be influenced by the Pre-Raphaelites. Even in this late work their influence can be seen in the choice of medieval subject and late Romantic style. The scene is from Malory's* Morte d'Arthur: *four British queens find the Arthurian hero asleep beneath an apple tree. The sorceress Morgan le Fay attempts to make him take one as a lover, but he remains faithful to Guinevere. Cowper contemporizes the subject by portraying the queens as 1950s starlets admiring a film star.*

RIGHT **Kilhwych, the King's Son** (*tempera on wood by Arthur Joseph Gaskin, 1862–1928). Gaskin's interest in the early Italian painters is evident in his use of tempera paint as well as in the curious perspective and flat forms seen here. This style was intentionally medieval, as was his choice of Arthurian subjects: Culhwch appears as a courtly huntsman from the Age of Chivalry. The great contrast between the finely attired prince and the homespun clothes of the whipper-in may reflect Gaskin's Socialist leanings.*

'What an affectionate greeting!' said Cei. 'If that log had been me, no one would ever have hugged me again.'

They entered the cottage and the strange woman gave them dinner. Afterwards they asked her about Olwen. 'The girl comes here every seven days to bathe and wash her clothes,' said the old woman, 'but you must swear not to do her any harm, for she is the fairest maiden in the kingdom.' And Olwen walked in. She wore a silken robe the colour of flaming fire with a collar of reddish gold, set with rubies and emeralds. Her hair was more golden than yellow broom flowers, and her skin was whiter than foam on the wave-crest. The fingers on her hands were fairer than the wood anemones that grow beside the spring. Her eyes glanced and gleamed like those of the falcon. Like the downy breast of the swan were her breasts, her cheeks were like red roses, and all who saw her felt great love for her. White three-leaved flowers sprang up in her footsteps, which led to her being named Olwen, meaning 'White Track'.

Culhwch told her of his love for her since he had heard her lovely name in childhood, and Olwen returned his love but told him that he must perform the tasks set by her father Yspaddaden, if he was to win her hand. Thereupon Olwen took Culhwch and his companies up to the castle and introduced them to Yspaddaden Pencawr, her royal father. 'Lift up the skin which has fallen over my eyes,' said Yspaddaden, 'so that I might see what kind of man desires to be my son-in-law.'

When Yspaddaden had seen Culhwch, he sent the group away after they had been promised an answer by the next morning; but as they walked off, the old king threw a poisoned dart at their backs. Bedwyr heard it whistling through the air, caught it, and hurled it back at Yspaddaden, catching him on the knee. 'Is that the way for a son-in-law to treat me?' cried the king. 'I shall have an eternal limp because of his discourtesy.'

The warriors returned to the cottage of Custennin the Giant, and the next day visited Yspaddaden for his decision. 'I must ask the permission of the four great-grandparents of Olwen,' said the king, but as they walked away he threw a second dart at them; this time it was Menw who returned the iron dart to its owner, piercing his breast. 'A curse on such an ungentlemanly son-in-law,' cried Yspaddaden. 'I shall never climb the hill again without a pain in my chest.'

On the following day the warriors once more sought an audience with Yspaddaden, and again he threw a dart at their backs. Culhwch caught it in the air and in a second the dart was through the eye of Yspaddaden and out the back of his head. 'I shall never see the same again,' said the king, 'due to the insolence of a son-in-law. A curse on the smith who forged the iron darts.' They sat down together to eat, and Yspaddaden turned to Cylhwch and said: 'So it is you who wishes for the hand of my daughter. Firstly you must swear never to unjustly harm me. Secondly you must bring to me whatever I ask of you. Only then shall my daughter be yours.'

'Make your request,' answered Culhwch.

'My hair and beard have not been cut for years,' said Yspaddaden, 'and the only comb, razor and scissors which will do the job are between the ears of the monstrous boar, Twrch Trwyth. Fetch me those implements and my daughter is yours. One word of advice I give you: enlist the help of Mabon the Hunter. Only he can hunt the boar with his dog Drudwyn; but no one has seen him since he was stolen from his mother when only three days old. You must find his kinsman Eidoel, who might be able to tell you where Mabon now dwells.'

Culhwch and the warriors of Arthur set out on the next stage of his quest. They soon found Eidoel who took them to seek the advice of an enchanted bird, the Ousel of Cilgwri. Gwrhyr, who knew the speech of birds, asked, 'Tell us where we can find Mabon, who was stolen from between the wall and his mother when only three nights in the world?'

'There was once', said the bird, 'a smith's anvil in this place, and I have pecked it for many years to reduce it to the size of a nut. But I swear that in all that time I have never heard of this Mabon. However, there is a race of beasts born long before my time; I shall take you to them.'

RIGHT **The 'Drosten' Stone** *(Pictish cross-slab from St Vigeans, Scotland; ninth century AD). The late Celtic art of the Picts continued earlier themes and styles. On the shaft of this Christian cross are the age-old subjects of mastery of animal over animal, and man over beast: an eagle clutches a salmon, while a hunter shoots at a wild boar. The spiralling lines of both the decorative and representational figures are continuing Celtic elements, expressed in a vigorous and naïve manner by the Pictish sculptors.*

The Ousel of Cilgwri thereupon led them to the Stag of Redynvre. 'We come to you, great stag,' said Gwrhyr, 'for we know of no animal older than you, and therefore perhaps you might know where we can find Mabon the Hunter.'

'There was once a great plain in this place,' replied the stag, 'and nothing grew on it save an oak sapling; that oak I have watched grow into a huge tree of one hundred branches, and I have watched it decay until now you see only a withered stump before you; and never in all that time have I heard of Mabon. But I shall take you to an even older creature than I,' and the Stag of Redynvre led them to the Owl of Cwm Cawlwyd.

'I would tell you if I knew,' said the owl to Gwrhyr, 'but when I first came to this broad valley it was a narrow wooded glen; a race of men were born who uprooted every tree. Since then two more woods have grown, and even so I have not heard of the man you are seeking. But let me take you to the oldest animal in the world, the Eagle of Gwern Abwy.'

'Many ages have passed since I came here,' said the eagle to Gwrhyr, 'and this rock was then so high that I could peck at the stars in the night; but now it is a span in height. But in all that time I have never heard mention of this Mabon. However, many years ago I was soaring above Llyn Llyw looking for food, and I spotted a salmon. I dived to catch it but it took me down into the depths and I scarcely managed to escape him. I returned to the lake with other eagles and he made his peace with me; I removed fifty fisherman's harpoons from his back as a sign of friendship. He must be older than I am, and I shall take you to where he lives in Llyn Llyw.'

The Eagle of Gwern Abwy led them to the Salmon of Llyn Llyw. 'I have come to visit you, old friend,' said the eagle, 'because these men are from the court of Arthur and they seek Mabon, the man who was snatched from between the wall and his mother when only three days old.'

'I can tell you this,' replied the salmon; 'with the turn of the tide I swim upstream as far as Gloucester, and there I find such evils; two of you must ride up with me on my back to witness what I see.' Cei and Gwrhyr volunteered and the salmon took them in leaps and dashes up to the city of Gloucester, where they heard loud cries from the castle dungeon beside the river.

'Who is it,' called Gwrhyr, 'that cries so mournfully from within this stone prison?'

'It is I, Mabon, the son of Modron!' was the reply.

LEFT **Olwen**
(*watercolour by Alan
Lee; 1981*). Olwen is
here depicted in the
midst of nature,
associated with the
Celtic Otherworld. The
side frames show the
warriors of Arthur's
court banqueting as they
discuss Culhwch's
request for the hand of
the unknown Olwen; in
the base-frame, warriors
ride out in search of the
giant's daughter.

ABOVE **Bronze boar from Bata, Hungary** *(second century* BC*). The wild boar remained a symbol of the warrior's ferocity throughout the pagan Celtic period. This figurine may have been worn as a helmet crest. The raised dorsal bristles symbolize the animal's aggression: in the myths, the hair of Celtic warriors similarly stands on end when they go into battle, and historians refer to the use of lime to make it bristle.*

The warriors returned to Arthur, who assembled his whole army to besiege the castle at Gloucester. During the battle Cei and Gwrhyr entered the dungeon from the river and rescued Mabon on the back of the salmon, and thereupon, Arthur called upon all the warriors of the islands of Britain to accompany them on the hunt for the boar, Twrch Trwyth. At that time it was living in Ireland with seven young pigs. The dogs were loosed upon the boar and they chased him until they reached the sea, a fifth of Ireland lain to waste behind them. Twrch Trwyth swam the sea to Wales, and Arthur and his companions followed boar and hounds to dry land. As the hunt progressed through Wales, one by one the seven pigs were killed, although the boar also killed many of Arthur's champions.

They came at last to the River Severn and the boar was about to swim across it to Cornwall when Mabon, son of Modron appeared. He rode at the boar and skilfully snatched the razor from between its ears. Cei likewise took the scissors, but the beast turned into the river estuary with the comb still safely lodged in the hair of its neck. It was on the shores of Cornwall that the comb was finally taken after a great struggle, and Twrch Trwyth disappeared into the deep sea, never to be seen again.

The warriors returned to the castle of Yspaddaden and cursed the king for the deaths he had caused. The king's beard was shaved right down to the bone.

'Is that a close enough shave?' asked Culhwch.

'It is,' said Yspaddaden, 'and my daughter is yours. But you would never have won her without help from Arthur for I would not have given her up of my own free will; and so I die as I lose her.'

In this way did Culhwch meet and take to wife Olwen, the daughter of Yspaddaden Pencawr.

OPPOSITE **Warriors with boar-crested helmets** *(bronze matrix for making decorative helmet plaques, from Torslunda, Sweden; eighth century* AD*). Cultural links between pre-Viking Scandinavia and the Celts are reflected in similar warrior aristocracies wearing similar armour: such boar crests are found in representations of Celtic warriors.*

Celtic Religion

Our understanding of Celtic religion is hindered, perhaps more than any other aspect of the Celtic world, by the lack of written sources and the difficulties involved in interpreting archeological evidence. These problems are increased by the secret nature of many Celtic religious cults, which was in part due to the great political respect commanded by Celtic priests and their consequent elitism.

Therefore we have to turn to the limited observations of ancient non-Celtic authors, whose writings are biased by their view of the Celts as primitive barbarians. The Greek Diodorus of Sicily, writing his 'mythical history' in the first century BC, refers (Book V, 31) to the high social status and learning of the Celtic Druids: 'Those men called by us philosophers and theologians are held in great honour by them; they call them "Druids" . . . and no sacrifice may be performed without a Druid present . . . for only they speak the language of the gods.' This Druidic control of religious affairs accounts for the many occasions in myth when they are consulted by clan-chiefs and kings – like ancient Greek oracles, they were able to influence political decisions. Julius Caesar tells us in his *Gallic War* (Book VI, 13–18) that the Druidic system originated in Britain and was exported to Gaul. He too refers to their great authority in Celtic society not only in religion, but also in educational and legal affairs, adding that their privileges included exemption from military service and taxation. Students of Druidic religion had to 'learn many verses by heart, sometimes for a period of 20 years. It is considered sacrilege to put their teachings into writing.' Celtic religion was thus *intended* to be mysterious and exclusive.

The importance of prophets in Celtic religion was also recorded by Diodorus: 'These men predict the future by observing the flight and calls of birds, and by the sacrifice of holy animals: all orders of society are in their power . . . and in very important matters they prepare a human victim, plunging a dagger into his chest; by observing the way his limbs convulse as he falls and the gushing of his blood, they are able to read the future.' Recent archeology has provided evidence to support such statements made by Greek and Roman writers that the Celts practised human

sacrifice. Excavations in the 1980s of a sacred Gallic site at Ribemont in Picardy, France, revealed pits filled with human bones, the thigh bones purposefully arranged into right-angled patterns. This sanctuary was levelled by Julius Caesar during his conquest of Gaul. The body of 'Lindow Man', recently discovered in a Cheshire peat bog (now in the British Museum in London), might also have been the victim of Druidic sacrifice.

The names of Celtic deities are known from references in later myths and from religious inscriptions of the Roman period in Gaul and Britain. However, there are several reasons why their natures and mythical 'biographies' remain elusive compared to the many surviving divine stories of other ancient cultures. Celtic artists rarely produced anthropomorphic (human) images before they came under Greek influence during the 'La Tène' period (between the third and the first centuries BC). Therefore the relatively late artistic representations of Celtic divinities, produced by artists trained in the Graeco-Roman style, are not very helpful in telling us about original Celtic perceptions of their gods. Likewise it is difficult to unravel information about pagan religious ritual from Celtic literature as Christian writers would later have adapted or omitted any blatant pagan elements. However, some scholars have argued that the underlying structures of many of the myths reflect their original significance in Druidic religious rituals, with the texts containing many significant pagan details.

Celtic divinities as well as religious rituals became intermingled with their Graeco-Roman counterparts during the period of Roman domination. Mercury, a god of merchants and 'inventor of all the arts', found his Celtic equivalent in Lugh, who in Irish mythology is called 'skilled in all the arts'. Animal gods were important in Celtic religion, and Epona, particularly revered as a horse goddess, was even worshipped by the Romano-British cavalry. Cernunnos ('the horned one') is connected not only with the stag, but with bulls, rams and other powerful male animals. Both hunter and protector of animals, Cernunnos has persisted in British folk traditions as Herne the Hunter.

Celtic goddesses and gods represented the elemental forces of nature, and according to classical writers, their shrines tended to be in secluded groves. Many of these sacred sites must have disappeared, and our knowledge of ritual activities is mainly limited to the monumentalized religious sanctuaries of the Roman period. Although

ABOVE **St Bride** (John Duncan; tempera on canvas, 1913). The pagan Celtic goddess Brigit was daughter of Dagda, one of the original Irish gods, the Tuatha de Danaan. Around AD 450 she was transformed into the Christian St Brigit, founder of the first nunnery at Kildare. A Scottish legend tells of her travelling from Iona to Bethlehem and returning with the baby Jesus. Duncan portrays her equally as the pagan bringer of Spring, being carried by angels across the Sound of Iona.

absolute evidence is lacking, Druidic religious rituals probably also took place at pre-Celtic monuments such as stone circles. The Celtic religious year revolved around the control of the seasons and nature by sun and moon, and topographical 'focuses' of worship were ordained. Thus the Irish Druids met at Visnech, the 'navel' of Ireland, and Stonehenge in the south of England may also have been such a centre.

The Celtic year was divided into summer and winter. Summer began on the first of May, after the feast of Beltain on May-Eve. During this festival in honour of 'the fire of Bel' (Irish Bile was an ancient god of life and death), domestic fires were extinguished and rekindled from a new Druidic fire. Winter began on the first of November, preceded by the feast of Samhain (our Hallowe'en) when, in Ireland, the Sidhe (fairies of the Otherworld) were believed to be abroad signalling the time of the dead.

EIGHT

Tristan and Isolt

The story of Tristan and Isolt has undergone many transformations since it first appeared in pagan Celtic times. Hundreds of different versions have been written since the medieval period, culminating in one of the greatest expressions of nineteenth century Romanticism, Wagner's opera Tristan and Isolde. Modern scholars have traced these later accounts back to two main medieval literary strands: the twelfth-century poetry of the Anglo-Norman Thomas d'Angleterre and the German Eilhart von Oberg, and the prose romances of thirteenth-century France. Two other twelfth-century versions, by the French poet Beroul (arguably the earliest surviving written account) and a short anonymous episode, Tristan's Madness, were not used by later authors. Each of these five early accounts probably derived from one original written version, no longer extant. This hypothetical first written version must have been the culmination of an oral tradition dating back to the pre-Christian Celtic storytellers.

The arguments for Celtic origin lie mainly in the topography of the story, which takes us through most of the early Celtic areas, although the episodes in later Celtic Brittany also suggest a post-Christian adaptation. The medieval accounts placed King Mark of Cornwall's castle at Tintagel, with its Arthurian connotations: by the thirteenth century the story had become part of mainstream Arthurian legend. Tristan's native country was Lyonesse in the early versions: tradition places this lost land off the coast of Cornwall, and there are many local Cornish legends of forests and tolling bells beneath the sea. Lyonesse might also have been a mythical name (it derives from the Celtic sun-deity Lugh) for the Pictish area of Lothian. Medieval literary patrons such as Eleanor of Aquitaine

encouraged their 'troubadours' to produce new versions of the old love stories which would both emphasize the contemporary ideology of 'courtly love', as well as bring them into line with current religious attitudes. The trend for 'medieval revivals' seen in nineteenth-century Europe inspired Romantic interpretations of the rediscovered poems. Wagner's main source was the German poem of Gottfried von Strassburg (c.1210), but the story had personal relevance to Wagner in reflecting his own love affair with his best friend's wife, Mathilde Wesendonck. Tennyson and other Victorian poets also produced versions of the story.

The underlying pagan Celtic nature of the story has never been lost: it is difficult to entirely Christianize or tame a story which deals with an adulterous love affair. Many even believe that the love potion was a post-Christian addition which provided an excuse for the lovers' sinful behaviour. However, it would seem likely that this is a Christian interpretation of an original Celtic feature as magical devices are common in Celtic mythology and reflect Druidic religious ritual. Ironically, the monks of Lindisfarne Priory still make a love potion from a secret recipe! The upbringing and heroic adventures of Tristan recall the deeds of the Irish CuChulainn and the Welsh Pryderi. Likewise, the strong and uncompromising characterization of Isolt and indeed the basic plot itself are paralleled in the stories of Irish Deirdre and Welsh Branwen. There is no 'authentic' version of Tristan and Isolt: major details of the plot differ from one account to another and the driving motives of the main characters vary according to the intentions of poet and audience. Some of the better known episodes are here incorporated into a prose version, omitting the blatantly Christian and medieval elements. However, some medieval French troubadour lays are included to enhance the narrative in the Celtic manner.

King Mark was ruler of Cornwall and dwelt in a fort at Tintagel, an impregnable stronghold on a high rocky promontory overlooking the Irish Sea. Cornwall was at war with Ireland and Mark's ally, Rivalin of Lothian, sailed down from Scotland to join in the struggle. As a sign of gratitude, Mark allowed Rivalin to return to Lothian with his sister as a wife. She died while giving birth to a son who, born in the midst of sorrow, was named Tristan.

Tristan was educated by Gorvenal, a wise and trusted member of Rivalin's court; the boy learnt all the arts of fighting and diplomacy, hunting and swimming. One day, when Tristan was sitting on the cliffs playing his harp to the sea birds, Gorvenal saw that the boy was ready: 'Young Tristan,' he said, 'I have taught you everything I know, and it

is time for you to see what lies beyond the bounds of Lothian.'

'But where shall I go?' asked Tristan.

'To where the winds blow you and to where your heart guides you.'

And Tristan, with his tutor Gorvenal as companion, sailed to the land of his mother in Cornwall. As they approached Tintagel Fort, Tristan turned to his men: 'None of you', he said, 'are to tell these noble people who I am. For if I am to be received by them, it must be out of respect for my behaviour and not my royal title.'

King Mark welcomed them honourably into his fort, and that evening invited them to the banquet. Once the wine was flowing he turned to his guests: 'Strangers,' he said, 'tell us who you are and from where you have come.'

ABOVE **Ornamented 'Q', the first letter of the Latin version of St Luke's Gospel** *(illuminated manuscript of the Gospels, Lindisfarne, Northumbria, England; c. 698 AD). Christian monks working in Celtic areas often ornamented their Christian manuscripts in a Celtic style; pagan monsters and human figures often appear among the interwoven patterns. The use of expensive colours such as gold and silver meant that the material value of these spiritual texts increased the likelihood of Viking raids on the monasteries.*

LEFT **Aerial view of Tintagel, Cornwall, England.** *The Lower Ward of the thirteenth-century castle is visible on the mainland (centre left). A modern bridge leads to a steep cliff-path which climbs up to the castle's Island Ward. On the summit of the Island are remains of the medieval Christian chapel. Archeologists have found evidence of an earlier, wealthy post-Roman stronghold on the Island contemporary with the 'Arthurian' Age, c. 450–600 AD). Local medieval legends associated the site with the birth of Arthur, while others saw it as King Mark's castle and the setting for tales of Tristan and Isolt.*

'We come from the north,' answered Tristan, 'and our fathers are merchants; but none of us has a heart for trading, and so we offer ourselves as warriors in your service.' Tristan then made music and the whole room fell quiet at the plaintive melodies of his harp.

'You shall stay here gladly,' said King Mark.

For over a year Tristan and his men from Lothian remained at Tintagel. The war with Ireland had ended with a treaty in which Mark had promised to send annual tribute to the King of Ireland. With the arrival of the warriors of Lothian Mark decided to refuse the payments, which consisted of the enslavement of young Cornish boys and girls, and thus came the chance that Tristan was waiting for to prove himself to the king.

A new champion had emerged in Ireland; he was Morholt, brother of the Irish queen and a great warrior. Tristan was the first to see Morholt's ship sailing towards Tintagel and he knew what he was coming for. Morholt beached his ship and sent a message to the king demanding the tribute. 'He shall not have it', said Tristan, 'without a fight.' As there were no other volunteers to meet Morholt in single combat, Mark agreed to Tristan's request to do so with a promise that he would be raised to the nobility of Cornwall if he succeeded.

Morholt accepted the challenge but on condition that his adversary was of equal royal bearing to himself.

FAR RIGHT **Door column of the Church of St Mary and St David, Kilpeck, near Hereford, England** *(twelfth century AD). Late Celtic warriors are interlaced with dragons in the pagan decorations of the Church exterior.*

RIGHT **Stone head** *(Salzburg, Austria; c. first century BC to first century AD). The Celts believed heads to contain magical properties: the heads of the enemy were greatly valued as battle-prizes and there are many mythical references to powerful heads. Carved stone heads probably had similar ritual significance.*

101

Tristan could no longer conceal his real identity from the court of Tintagel: 'I am the son of King Rivalin of Lothian,' he said, 'and nephew to King Mark of Cornwall.' King Mark was at once happy and sad that this fine young man was his sister's son, and yet he was to risk his life for Cornwall. Tristan, however, would not be dissuaded and it was agreed that the fight would take place on a small island opposite Tintagel.

At dawn on the appointed day, Tristan rowed out towards the island, and seeing Morholt's boat drawn up on the beach, he abandoned his own and waded ashore. Morholt was clearly puzzled by this behaviour: 'Why did you push your boat out to sea?' he asked.

'Only one of us will be leaving this island today,' answered Tristan, drawing his sword and striking the first blow.

The sea birds were the only witnesses to the long and bloody battle. The final blow was struck by Tristan: his sword smashed through Morholt's helmet, splitting his skull. Morholt was taken from the island in the Irish ship, while Tristan rowed the small boat back to Tintagel where there was much rejoicing that night. But Tristan was strangely troubled: his sword had splintered and a small fragment was missing.

Morholt died on the sea voyage home and there was great mourning in Ireland for the death of their hero.

The king's daughter, whose name was Isolt, had been taught the magic properties of herbs by her mother. While attempting to revive Morholt with her craft, she extracted a piece of sharp metal from his fractured head. She wrapped it in silk knowing that one day she would discover the sword from which it came: on that day she would avenge her uncle.

Tristan had suffered a small wound from Morholt's spear, but did not realise at first that it had been dipped in one of the poisons brewed by Isolt of Ireland. The wound began to fester and soon no one would approach Tristan's room for the stench. Tristan knew that the antidote for the poison lay somewhere across the sea and he had himself pushed out into the ocean where he drifted for many days. Manannan the Sea God watched over him and blew his boat gently towards Ireland. When the land came into view Tristan took up his harp and sang. The people of Dublin were amazed at the sight of the boat without a pilot. As it drew nearer they heard the soft sounds of a sweet harp playing and a voice singing. The music enchanted them and they drew the boat ashore and carried the wounded minstrel, who called himself Tantris, to the court. There he was tended by the maids of Princess Isolt and cured by her herbs: but the two never met before it came time for Tristan to return to Cornwall.

LEFT **Iron-Age settlement, Chysauster, Cornwall, England** (c. first century BC to third century AD). The well-preserved remains of nine 'courtyard houses' at Chysauster reveal a stone-paved passage leading into an open courtyard, off which open several small rooms. Originally with thatched roofs, the houses had drains and terraced gardens.

ABOVE **Warrior fights monster** (*bronze matrix for making decorative helmet plaques, from Torslunda, Sweden; eighth century* AD). *The* Teutonic warriors of pre-Viking Sweden, like their Celtic neighbours, decorated their helmets with scenes of power. Here, a warrior with axe confronts a wild beast.

103

In Cornwall, he had long been given up for dead and great was the rejoicing at his homecoming; but there were some in Mark's court who were jealous of the affection which the foreigner Tristan had inspired in their king, and they planned to find Mark a wife, in the hope that a son would be born and inherit Cornwall. The king was aware of their schemes and one day found a reason for putting off the marriage for ever. It was early summer and Mark was sitting by a window looking out to sea. The swallows were swooping low over the cliffs and one of them dropped a ruddy golden thread into his lap. Mark ran it through his fingers and realized that it was a woman's hair. At the feast that evening Mark held up the long fair hair: 'Many of you,' he said, 'wish to see me married; but I shall marry no one except the owner of this hair. There will be great rewards for the man who discovers her and brings her back to Cornwall.'

'I killed Morholt for you,' said Tristan, 'and I shall find you a wife.'

Tristan set sail from Tintagel with his friends and Manannan blew up a great storm which shipwrecked them on the coast near Dublin. The men of Lothian disguised themselves as merchants and stood around in the markets listening out for clues to the owner of the golden hair; but the news was not of women but of dragons. The countryside around Dublin was being devastated by a fire-breathing monster and the King of Ireland had offered the hand of his daughter Isolt to the man who brought him evidence of the creature's death. Tristan instinctively set out to find the dragon, following the scorched earth towards its lair, where he sat and waited for the monster's return.

Tristan was gazing at the full moon when against it appeared the black shadow of the dragon. The air grew hot as it approached and Tristan caught sight of it in the moonlight as it flew towards the den. It was a white dragon with huge flapping wings and a long pointed rail; along its spine ran a line of poisonous thorns and its teeth gleamed razor-sharp. Tristan confronted the monster which roared and shot out billows of white smoke from its nostrils, enshrouding him in a mist. Tristan could see nothing until suddenly the clouds were broken by the dragon's opening jaws. Tristan's reactions were fast and he plunged his spear into its throat, performed the salmon leap onto its neck and reached over to slice off the dragon's poisonous forked tongue. He put the tongue inside his stocking and set off for Dublin; but the warmth of his body drew out the poison and Tristan collapsed on the path which led to the dragon's lair.

The Irish king's steward, who secretly lusted after Isolt, had been watching the whole battle from a tree; he hacked off the dragon's head and took it to the King, claiming his prize. Isolt shrank at the thought of marrying this man, who was considered a liar and coward by many in the court. Therefore she went with her mother and Brangaine, her maidservant, to the dragon's lair; there they found Tristan unconscious, with the forked tongue in his hand, and they carried him between them back to the court. Brangaine then recognized him as Tantris, the minstrel they had tended months earlier, and Tristan continued to hide his true identity.

It was several weeks before Tristan began to recover with the help of Isolt's herbs. Isolt had become increasingly attracted to this stranger, who even on his sick-bed played the harp so beautifully. It seemed curious to her that such a minstrel should also be a valiant fighter, and she hoped in her heart of hearts that he would survive the dragon's poison and claim her as his prize.

The day came for him to leave his bed and while he was bathing Isolt cleaned his armour. The notch on his sword caught her notice and she ran to her room to find the silk-wrapped

LEFT **Gaullish prisoner** (c. *first century* BC). *This Roman bronze depicts the Celt as a stereotyped heroic enemy, hands tied behind back. Trousers were favoured by Celtic chieftains from the Hallstatt period onwards, whereas Irish aristocrats wore knee-length tunics and cloaks. Aristocratic Celtic women also wore tunics and cloaks.*

105

splinter which not so long ago she had removed from her uncle's head: the piece perfectly fitted the notch in the minstrel's sword. At that moment Isolt's feelings of love for Tristan turned to hatred. 'So at last the gods have brought you to me,' she said to him. 'You are the man who slew my uncle Morholt. On that mournful day when I realized that my herbs had no power over death, I swore that one day I would have my revenge.'

'I killed Morholt in single combat,' said Tristan, 'and on behalf of my king. There was no treachery in your uncle's death, but treachery will triumph if you kill me, for then you must marry the steward who lays claim to the dragon-slaying. I am the only man who can prove him false.' And Isolt stormed out of the room, and neither of them could sleep that night.

The next day the court gathered to hear the steward make his official claim to Isolt. 'It was no easy task,' he said holding up the dragon's head, 'but I suffered no wounds and will defend you equally well when the next monster arrives.'

'You are that lying monster,' cried Isolt, 'and here is the man who truly killed the dragon.' Tristan was led into the hall.

'Prove it!' spat the steward.

'This coward has the head,' said Tristan, 'but I have the deadly tongue. I am Tristan, royal nephew of the King of Cornwall. I was sent here to find the owner of this golden hair, and I think that in killing the dragon, I have found her.' And Tristan held up the dragon's tongue in one hand and the hair in the other. Every man and woman present gasped, for the tongue was hideous and the hair beautiful: and every head turned from the cowering steward to the Princess Isolt.

'Your king shall have Isolt as his queen,' said the Irish king, 'and let this marriage bind a peace between our two countries.' The day before they left for Cornwall, Isolt's mother gave a powerful love potion to Brangaine: 'You are to slip half of this into the King of Cornwall's wine, and half into my daughter's on their wedding night. It will surely bind them together in love.'

The ship sailed out of Dublin harbour and Isolt stood at the stern and watched the sun setting in reds and golds over her land as it slipped away from her. For two days the sea was whipped up by the storm chariots of Manannan the Sea God; by the third day the winds had died away and the ship was strangely becalmed. The sun beat down on Tristan and Isolt as they played a board game to pass away the time: Isolt still would not speak to Tristan. She called Brangaine to fetch them a refreshing herbal drink from her travelling-chest. They drank, as was the custom, from the same bowl; and as they drank the winds blew and the sail filled, the waves lashed and the salt spray was in their hair. Their hands touched as they passed the bowl from one to the

ABOVE **Fight of the Red and White Dragons** (The St Alban's Chronicle, Lambeth Palace Library, London, England; fifteenth century AD). The fifth-century AD British leader of history, Vortigern, had become a semi-mythical character by the time of the twelfth-century author, Geoffrey of Monmouth. He recounts a traditional tale concerning a prophetic vision of two fighting dragons. The manuscript illustration seen here depicts Ambrosius (the Arthurian Merlin) explaining the meaning to Vortigern: the red dragon (representing Celtic Britain) defeats the white one (the invading Saxons).

BELOW **Bronze boar statuette** (*Hounslow, Middlesex, England; first century BC to first century AD*). *The figure was found together with other boars and a wheel, which were perhaps votive offerings to a sun god at a Celtic shrine. Like other Celtic boars, its dorsal spine is emphasized: the animal was a symbol of virility, which was signified in myth and reality by the warrior's bristling hair.*

other, at first shyly and then with the full passion that the draught inspired: for Brangaine had mistakenly served them with the love potion.

The ship arrived at Tintagel and King Mark was highly pleased with Isolt. But it was not Isolt that he slept with on their wedding night. Tristan realized that the King would discover that he was not the first to make love to Isolt: therefore he persuaded Brangaine to slip into the marriage bed the moment the lights were extinguished. Thus began the many deceits that were to lead eventually to the discovery of Tristan and Isolt's secret love, for the lovers could not keep away from one another, try as they might. Both Tristan and Isolt felt much guilt, for each of them felt great affection towards Mark, but the love potion's magic was intended to last for three years and it was too strong for them to resist.

Those that had always been jealous of Tristan now found a way of putting him out of favour. It was not difficult for them to arouse the king's suspicions for Tristan and Isolt were ever flirting across the table at ban-quets. One man in particular, Andret, who had a secret desire for Isolt, hoped that one day the lovers would be discovered. The rumours grew and Mark expelled Tristan from the court. Even so, Tristan and Isolt could not be parted. There was a spring in the orchard outside the walls of Tintagel which flowed as a stream into the fort; Tristan would hide up a tree in the orchard and throw summer flowers or twigs in winter into the stream as a sign to Isolt that he was waiting for her. Andret asked a Druid to determine from the stars whether the two were still seeing one another. The Druid saw it all in the night sky: the orchard, the flowers in the stream and Isolt slipping out of the fort.

One day the Druid predicted that a lover's tryst was to take place while the king was out hunting the wild boar that night. Andret therefore schemed to bring the king back home earlier than expected at the following dawn. Tristan and Isolt met among the night-scented flowers of the orchard while Brangaine kept watch as usual from the tower above Isolt's chamber. As the first glimmers

of dawn were touching the starry sky Brangaine sang:

'God of light which makes
    things true and clear,
Please be faithful and help my
    companions,
For I have not seen them
    since twilight
And before long will it be
    dawn.

'Fine companions, whether
    you sleep or are waking,
Sleep no more, my masters, if
    you please.
For in the eastern sky the star
    ascends
Which heralds the day which
    I knew would come,
And before long will it be
    dawn.

'Fine companions, my song is
    calling you,
Sleep no more, for I hear the
    bird singing
As it looks for the day
    amongst the thickets.
And I fear that the jealous
    man is after you,
And before long will it be
    dawn.'

Tristan returned her song:

'Beautiful sweet companion,
    so rich is this place,
That I wish that it would
    never be dawn or day.
For the woman I hold in my
    arms
Is the most beautiful ever
    born of a mother,
And that is why I care so
    little
For the jealous fool and the
    dawn . . .'

Tristan's song was interrupted by King Mark and his warriors, who had crept into the orchard guided by Andret. The two lovers were bound and immediately their punishment was pronounced: Tristan and Isolt

were to be burnt in a pit of flaming branches. On their way to the place of death, Tristan was allowed to make an offering of appeasement to the angry gods on a sacred rock above the sea. 'Save yourself!' cried Isolt. 'If you live then I shall also live in death.' And Tristan leapt into the sea; so high was the cliff that all who saw him jump considered him dead. The only sound was the crying of sea gulls.

'A fine sacrifice to Manannan the Sea God,' said Mark, and Isolt was taken to the death-pit. A group of diseased men who lived in the woods surrounding Tintagel approached the place. 'Since Queen Isolt is to die anyway,' said one of them, his face

ABOVE **Distant view of the headland at Tintagel, Cornwall, England.** *The legendary birthplace of King Arthur was also believed in local folklore to have been the fortress of King Mark. Tintagel was its medieval name, meaning 'The Fortress of the Constriction' and taken from the Celtic words* din *(fort) and* tag *(obstruct or construct). An apt description for the dramatic manner in which the Island meets the mainland.*

hideously pock-marked, 'why not give her to us for our pleasure. She will soon be dead, and her death will appease the evil demons who bring disease to your lands.' And Isolt was unbound and taken away.

Tristan had survived his plunge into the sea and lay in ambush for the captors of Isolt as they took her away to the woods. He had no difficulty in saving her from them, and Tristan and Isolt lived as outlaws in the woods for many months. The effects of the love potion, which had been brewed to last for three years, were wearing off: they had shared a beautiful dream and were waking into a world of harsh reality. Their love for one another became real, but so did their strong sense of remorse for having wounded the heart of King Mark. Tristan decided that he must leave Cornwall for Brittany; and Isolt returned to Tintagel and swore an oath of loyalty to her husband. Soon Isolt saw from her tower a small boat sailing southwards along the coast; and she knew that she would never see Tristan alive again.

Tristan landed in Brittany with his companion Gorvenal, and they offered themselves as warriors to the local king, whose name was Hoel. Tristan, who no longer cared whether he lived or died, immediately proved his courage in battle against a neighbouring tribe. That evening at the victory banquet, King Hoel stood up and announced: 'Today I have seen a new hero who is quite reckless in battle; as a reward I offer him my daughter, Isolt of the White Hands, as a wife.' Tristan was now as reckless in his drinking as he was at fighting. He looked at Isolt of the White Hands who had blushed the colour of the foxglove on the moor, reminding him of another Isolt. That night they slept together, but Tristan could not bring himself to make love to a distant heart. His excuse was that he was suffering from an old wound.

Isolt of the White Hands tolerated her husband's lack of interest and even began to joke about it with her maidservants. One day she was out hunting with her brother Kaherdin; as they were jumping a fence the mud splashed up and spattered her thighs: 'Why!' she laughed, 'even the mud is more interested in me than my husband.' And that evening Kaherdin questioned Tristan and discovered the real reason for his coldness; Tristan swore Kaherdin to silence by promising that he would make every effort to forget his former love.

The following day brought a surprise attack on Hoel's fort and Tristan was badly wounded. Isolt of the White Hands did not have the potent herbal cures of Isolt the Fair (as the men of Brittany called the Cornish queen). Tristan, realizing that he was going to die unless Isolt herself came to him, gave a message to Gorvenal to take to Cornwall: 'Tell the men of Cornwall that I am dying of a poisoned wound, and that only Queen Isolt can cure me. Go in my boat and if you return with Isolt, hoist the white sail, but if she will not come, then let the sail be black.' Isolt of the White Hands overheard the message and at last knew where Tristan's absent heart lay.

Several days later Tristan had become very weak and was on the threshold of the Underworld; suddenly he heard the watchmen of King Hoel's fort shouting that a boat was in view. 'What colour is the sail?' he asked his Breton wife. Isolt of the White Hands felt the jealousy well up inside her: 'It is black, my lord,' she replied. Tristan's heart burst within him as Isolt the Fair and King Mark came running into his room. Isolt stood above her dead lover and, hearing the sounds of his harp in her memory, sang:

'The sun is shining, clear and
    fair,
And I can hear the sweet
    song of birds;
All around me they sing in
    the thickets
And their songs are new.

BELOW **Head of the Celtic god Coriosolites** (*bronze coin from Brittany; first century* BC). *The Celts borrowed the idea of coinage from the Greeks and Romans; local kings portrayed themselves on the coins, together with symbols of their trade and wealth on the reverse, such as ears of corn or horses. This Gallic coin depicts a local god, with fashionable Celtic warrior hairstyle: note the chain with a severed head attached hanging from his hair. Diodorus refers to the Celtic custom of taking heads as proof of valour in battle, and such heads were sometimes offered to warrior gods.*

RIGHT **Gold boat model** (*from Broighter, County Derry, Ireland; first century* BC). *This miniature boat, complete with benches, mast and oars, was part of a hoard of gold jewellery and may have been an offering to a water deity such as the Irish sea god, Manannan.*

'I see my own death coming,
And I sing a lay which will be
   held most dear,
And will not fail to touch
   lovers,
For it is love which makes me
   long to die.

'Tristan, my friend, friend,
   friend,
Here is my heart which I
   entrusted
To your love; not a good
   place for it,
and now it will die by your
   sword.

'Tristan, my friend, friend,
   friend,
Even though the gods despise
   my desire,
My soul shall dwell in your
   spirit,
In the lands of the blessed or
   in the Underworld.'

Falling on Tristan's sword, Isolt
followed him to the Underworld, and
thus did the lovers return in death to
King Mark's fort at Tintagel. They
were buried in two mounds, side by
side, and the intertwining branches of
two trees grew from their graves.

Folktales and Songs From Around the Celtic World

CORNWALL

Cornwall was a stronghold of Romano-Celtic culture until the Saxon invasions and not surprisingly it is the birthplace of many Arthurian legends, including that of Tristan and Isolt. Until recently, the river Tamar was regarded by the Cornish people as a cultural boundary between the Cornish and the English. The Cornish language was related to Breton, but was extinct by the nineteenth century. However, Cornish folk-singers such as Brenda Wooton have kept the poetic language alive, and recently there have been attempts at revival. This poem appeared in the Cornish language in the seventeenth century. It originates in an earlier English folk song. Strawberry water was once a favourite skin toner. The bold replies of the girl continue the Celtic mythological tradition of feminine pride.

'Where lies your path,
      lovely girl,' he said,
'with your flaxen locks, and
      your face so pale?'
'I go to the spring, kind sir,'
      said she,
'with strawberry leaves, I'll
      never fail.'

'May I come too, lovely girl,'
      he said,
'with your flaxen locks, and
      your face so pale?'
'If that is your wish, kind
      sir,' said she,
'with strawberry leaves, I'll
      never fail.'

'And what if I lay you on the
      grass,
with your flaxen locks, and
      your face so pale?'
'I'll rise up again, kind sir,'
      said she,
'with strawberry leaves, I'll
      never fail.'

'And what if you find
      yourself with child,
with your flaxen locks, and
      your face so pale?'
'I'll carry that child, kind
      sir,' said she,
'with strawberry leaves, I'll
      never fail.'

'What man will be there to
      hold the child,
with your flaxen locks, and
      your face so pale?'
'You'll be the father, kind
      sir,' said she,
'with strawberry leaves, I'll
      never fail.'

'With what will you clothe
      this child of yours,
with your flaxen locks, and
      your face so pale?'
'From the father's thread,
      kind sir,' said she,
'with strawberry leaves, I'll
      never fail.'

THE ISLE OF MAN

The island's position in the Irish Sea between Ireland and Scotland has ensured it a place in Celtic mythology and tradition. It may have been considered one of the Isles of the Blessed, as was the island of Arran, ruled by the archaic Irish God of the Sea, Manannan (another child of Lir). The Manx language, closely related to Scottish Gaelic, was considered extinct by the 1950s, but there have been recent attempts at revival. An oral traditon of law, which might reflect original Druidic practice, had precedence, until recently, over written laws. Post-Celtic man was governed by Vikings until Scottish rule began in the thirteenth century. The following Manx folk–song has Christian references, but its themes of love vows, curses and powerful natural elements are those of Celtic mythology.

I first met my truelove at the Christmas ceilidh; we sat while the fiddler played and began our courting.

For seven whole years we met and made love, and her unfaithful tongue swore that she would never leave me.

On the Sunday before Ash Wednesday I visited by truelove; she placed her hands over mine and swore she would marry only me.

I came home in ecstasy, everything was roses; on the Wednesday I heard she had married another.

I cursed her for courting me for so long a time; when she found she had no love for me she should have said so.

But I cannot speak wickedly of her or call for bad luck; may she make her new friends glad, though love has a made a fool of me.

No one knew about our love save the old walnut tree; it cannot speak for me though it knows my lover false.

On St Patrick's Day I shall visit the fair in my young man's clothes, I'll walk right by her, pretending not to notice.

At the fair I'll take my pick from all the best girls; but she has no second chance with her deceitful new husband.

I walked the long winding road and grew weary of the slopes, but whenever I rested I thought of my love.

I wish that the wind would bring me news of my love; I wish she would cross the steep highlands to greet me and meet me by the shore.

How happily I would run to the shore if she were there; how happily my hand would make a pillow for her hair.

I wish that the sea would run dry and let me have my way; but the white snows of Greenland will sooner turn the red of roses before I forget my truelove.

LEFT **Madron Well,
Cornwall, England.**
*Sources of water were
revered by the Celts for
their religious powers,
and many of these
sacred springs and wells
continued to be visited
for spiritual healing in
the Christian era, often
dedicated to saints.
Madron was also the
site of a baptistry. Sick
people still drink these
waters and hang votive
rags on the surrounding
trees.*

BRITTANY

*I*n the fifth century, several noble Welsh families fled the Saxon invasion of their country and landed in France. The area later became known as 'Little Britain' or Brittany. The Bretons brought their Celtic language and mythology with them, but many of their stories have been lost owing to the French government's past ban on speaking Breton. Only folk-tales and songs have survived in the Breton tongue: the Breton singer and harpist, Alan Stivell, has led the recent revival. The following traditional ballad contains a reference to the Virgin Mary, but the common ancient Celtic theme of the sea as a setting for miraculous tales involving women is present in the song. It was collected from the singing of Janet ar Gall of Kerarborn in 1849.

It was the first of November when the English reached Dourduff.
They beached at Dourduff and snatched a young girl.
They snatched a lovely maiden and took her to their ship.
Her name was Marivonnik and she came from Plougasnou.
As they carried her away, she cried at her father's door:

'Fare thee well dear mother and father, for I'll never see you more.
'Fare thee well dear brother and sister, for we'll never meet on earth.
'Fare thee well kinsmen and friends, for I'll never see your world again.'
And young Marivonnik wept, with no one there to comfort her.
No one was there to comfort her save the big Englishman, he comforted her.
'Do not cry, my Marivonnik, your life is not at risk;
'Your life is not at risk, but I cannot save your honour.'
'Sir Englishman, my honour means more to me than all your ships at sea;
'Tell me then, shall I lose my honour to more than you alone?'
'To me and to my cabin boy, and to the sailors if they want you.
'To my sailors if they want you, every one hundred and one.'
'Tell me then, Sir Englishman, may I walk with you on the bridge?'
'You may walk up on the bridge, but take care not to drown.'
Young Marivonnik cried, whilst walking on the deck:
'Help me, Mary Virgin, shall I end it all by drowning?
'It is for you, dear Virgin Mary, so as not to offend you.
'If I fall in the sea, then drowned I shall be; if I stay I shall be killed.'
Young Marivonnik was guided by the Virgin and dived into the sea.
She was brought back to the surface by a small fish.
The big Englishman then called out to his sailormen:
'Sailors, sailors, rescue her and five hundred crowns are yours!'
And later that day he told young Marivonnik:
'You should not have done this, Marivonnik, for you were to be my wife.'

WALES

The Welsh language has survived in education and broadcasting, though what chance it stands against the English and American mass-media remains to be seen. The Mabinogion *and Arthurian legends have survived in folk–tales as well as in high literature. The following story appears in the* Journey Through Wales *by the twelfth–century church-man, Giraldus Cambrensis. In that Christianized version, Elidor is training to be a monk and runs away from his harsh teachers: I have omitted the Christian elements. The modern English author Alan Garner sets the story in Manchester where the escape is from urban squalor. The theme of the visit to the fairy world is one of the commonest in Celtic mythology. Such myths also provided the Celts with an 'explanation' for the great tomb mounds of the earlier Bronze–Age culture. The 'yellow ball' in this story is a fairy flower in other versions, all of which contain the feature of the fairy rule that you may not take anything back with you to the mortal world.*

Elidor was a young boy who was fed up with life. One day on the way to school he turned around and made his way to the woods. He wandered along the river in a dream and soon found himself at the entrance to a cave. Two little people came running out and said: 'Why don't you come inside and have some fun? Our world is happier than yours!'

Elidor did not stop to think, but followed them into the cave and found himself in a dark passageway which became narrower and lower until he was squeezing through on all fours. Just as he was beginning to panic the tunnel opened out into another cavern; they made for the light at the entrance and Elidor emerged into a world which he had only ever seen in paintings and dreams. It was an idyllic landscape with flowery meadows running down to lazy rivers; and yet there was something wrong too — Elidor looked up and saw that, although the world was bright, there was a mist hanging over everything so that neither sun, moon nor stars would shine.

Elidor was led before the king who asked who he was and from where he had come. The king was rather confused by the boy's answers and waved

RIGHT **Snowdonia.** *The highland region of north-west Wales has proved a difficult obstacle for Roman and English invaders. Many Welsh myths are located in the region, which provides a dramatic backdrop of lakes, streams and mountains.*

him away saying, 'You will remain here as a playmate for my son.' That afternoon, if indeed it was afternoon, Elidor stood back and watched the little people as they played. They were finely proportioned and most had long fair hair. Their riding was on horses the size of greyhounds, but they did not hunt for they did not eat meat, preferring milk flavoured with saffron. In their conversations they ridiculed Elidor's people for their lives of violence and deceit, yet they did not have any religious beliefs.

Elidor grew homesick and the king allowed him a visit to his mother on condition that he returned. The little people led him back into the cavern, through the cramped tunnel which became wider and higher, until they reached the cave by the river. Here Elidor left his tiny companions and returned to his mother's house. She asked him where he had been and begged him not to leave home again, but he told her of his promise to the king. Thus Elidor spent his time divided between the ordinary world and the land of the little people.

One day Elidor told his mother of the brilliant yellow balls that they played with in the other place. His mother asked him to bring one home for she was poor and thought that they must be golden. So the next time Elidor was playing with the little people he took one of the balls and ran off with it into the cavern, through the widening passage and back to his mother. But just as he entered the house a tiny foot tripped him up and he dropped his treasure. He turned just in time to see the two little people scowl at him and run off with the ball.

The following day Elidor went into the woods and walked along the river to the cave, but he could no longer find it. Many years later he would walk along the river with his own children and tell them again and again the story of the little people.

LEFT **A Spirit or Sidhe in a Landscape** (*oil on board by George William Russell, 1867–1935). The Irish artist's play Deirdre was performed in Dublin in 1902, and he is best known as a poet of works based on Celtic mythology. As a painter he tended to concentrate on a particular theme during a particular period. Between 1900–1905 he produced a series of images of Celtic spirits in landscape settings.*

SCOTLAND

*T*he original Celtic inhabitants of Scotland north of the rivers Forth and Clyde were known by the fourth century as Picti ('Painted Ones'). The Picts were probably given this nickname by the Roman soldiers guarding Hadrian's Wall to describe their tattooed bodies. Archeologists have found tattoos on preserved Celtic flesh and ancient writers tell us that they painted their bodies. The Scotti ('Irishmen') came to Argyll from the kingdom of Dalriada in Antrim, Ireland, bringing their Irish Gaelic language to Scotland. In the ninth century the Scots took over the Pictish areas and it is their Gaelic language which still survives in parts of the Highlands and Hebrides. The land of Scotland features in many of the ancient Irish myths and legends and the Scottish folk-tales and local legends which have survived are mainly from the later Gaelic tradition. The following folk–tale looks back to the ancient period.

*S*ome say that the Picts knew the recipe for the brewing of heather-ale. The secret was passed down from father to son for many centuries, but was finally lost when the Scots invaded the Pictish kingdom in the ninth century. The story goes as follows. The Scots loved the heather-ale which they imported from the Picts, and they longed to have the secret recipe. The family who guarded the recipe lived in the Mull of Galloway in the far west of the Pictish kingdom. One day father and son were captured in battle and the Scots had them brought out onto the open moor high up above the sea where the purple heather used for the famous brew was growing all around them. The Scots demanded the recipe, threatening and torturing the old man and his young son until they were on the point of death.

RIGHT **Horseman drinking** *(Pictish stone from Invergowrie, near Dundee, Scotland; c. ninth century* AD*). The native Celtic Picts were probably a continuation of the Caledonian tribes who resisted the Roman invasion. Together with the intrusive Irish Scotti, they invaded the Roman territory of northern Britain in the fourth and fifth centuries* AD*. The Pictish Kingdom controlled northern Britain between the sixth and ninth centuries, and eventually joined with the Scotti in the formation of Scotland. Horses were status symbols in all Celtic societies; here, the rider drinks from a horn which, with its eagle-headed terminal, is a further symbol of power.*

The sea-gulls were mewing as dusk began to fall. 'I shall tell you what you want to know,' spoke the old man at last, 'but only on condition that you first kill my son, so that he does not have the pain of witnessing his father bring dishonour and shame to our people.' The weary Scots raised a cry of victory and the boy was put to the sword. 'Now, old man,' they said, 'tell us the recipe.'

'Ha!' said the father, 'do you really think I would tell a Scot the secret of heather-ale? My son was about to divulge the recipe, for he still had many years to live and would not readily give up this beautiful world of sea-birds, high cliffs and the sounds of the foaming sea. Therefore he had to die; and the secret of heather-ale dies with him, for you will never have it from me!'

The Scottish chieftain was furious. 'Take him,' he cried, 'and hurl him from the highest cliff. Let him be smashed to pieces on the sharp rocks below, and may the sea mourn him forever more with her salty tears.'

Thus the old man died, and now shares the secret of heather-ale with the sea.

RIGHT **Christy Moore.** *The Irish singer/songwriter continues the tradition of the Celtic bards by heroizing the modern freedom-fighters of Ireland and Central America. He has sung with the Irish folk group Planxty as well as with Moving Hearts, one of the earliest bands to combine folk, rock and jazz styles. Here he is playing the Irish bodhran, a hand-held drum.*

IRELAND

*F*or historical reasons the Celtic tradition has survived better in Ireland than in any of the other Celtic areas. Modern Irish Gaelic is a close descendant of the ancient Celtic language; it is still spoken in the southwest and was recognized as an official language by the Republic of Ireland in 1921. Many Celtic myths and legends have come down to us in Irish, and the Irish folk-tale tradition is equally strong. The following traditional ballad was first sung at the time of the mass emigrations to America by young Irish men and women seeking work after the Great Famine of the 1840s. This relatively* modern song is addressed to the legendary heroes of Ireland, a typical use of myth to conjure up a distant Golden Age. The emigrations themselves have now become legendary and the mythical power of the song remains relevant in a country still affected by emigration; it was recently recorded in 1983 by the Irish band Planxty.*

You brave Irish heroes
wherever you be,
I pray stand a moment and
listen to me,
Your sons and fair daughters
are now going away,
And thousands are sailing to
Americay.

So good luck to those people
and safe may they land,
They are leaving their
country for a far distant
strand,
They are leaving old Ireland,
no longer can stay,
And thousands are sailing to
Americay.

The night before leaving they
are bidding goodbye,
And it's early next morning
their heart gives a sigh,
They do kiss their mothers
and then they will say
'Farewell, dear old father, we
must now go away.'

Their friends and relations
and neighbours also,
When the trunks are all
packed up, all ready to go,
O the tears from their eyes
they fall down like the
rain,
And the horses are prancing,
going off for the train.

So good luck to those people
and safe may they land,
They are leaving their
country for a far distant
strand,
They are leaving old Ireland,
no longer can stay,
And thousands are sailing to
Americay.

When they reach the station,
you will hear their last cry,
With handkerchiefs waving
and bidding goodbye,
Their hearts will be breaking
on leaving the shore,
'Farewell, dear old Ireland,

will we ne'er see you
more?'

O I pity the mother that rears
up the child,
And likewise the father who
labours and toils,
To try to support them he
will work night and day,
And when they are older they
will go away.

So good luck to those people
and safe may they land,
They are leaving their
country for a far distant
strand,
They are leaving old Ireland,
no longer can stay,
And thousands are sailing to
Americay.

ENGLAND

---

*I*n spite of the various invasions of
England from the Roman times onwards, there are still folk memories of the
Celtic past when the Brythonic language
was spoken. England has a good number
of pagan Celtic folk-customs, from the
corn dolly to Morris Dancing. Un-
Christianized Arthurian legends have
persisted in local folklore and many
English folk–songs appear to stem back
to a pagan Celtic origin.

The 'high' subject matter of the
following ballad suggests that it was
composed for the court, but the col-
loquial language points to its later
transformation into folk-song. The court
bards were travellers and their songs
were often heard by rich and poor alike.
The song contains typical Celtic themes:
the wife from across the sea and the
problems of cultural integration. The use
of magic spells to forestall a royal birth
has its counterpart in the Greek myth of
Herakles, where a similarly jealous but
divine wife sends the goddess of childbirth

King Willy he's sailed over
    the raging foam,
He's wooed a wife and he's
    brought her home.
He wooed her for her long
    golden hair,
His mother wrought her a
    mighty care:
And a weary spell she's laid
    on her,
She be with child full long
    and many's the year,
But her child she would never
    bear.
And in her bower she lies in
    pain,
King Willy at her bedhead he
    do stand
As down his cheeks the
    salten tears do run.

King Willy back to his
    mother he did run,
And he's gone there as a
    begging son.
He says: 'My truelove has this
    fine noble steed
'The like of which you ne'er
    did see:
'At every part of this horse's
    mane
'There's hanging fifty silver

ABOVE **Corn-dolly seller, Lyme Regis, Dorset, England.** *The Celts relied heavily on agriculture, and many sacrificial rituals were linked to the continuing fertility of the land. Until recently, the last sheaves of corn during harvest used to be plaited into figures or talismans which contained the spirits of the corn. The associated religious ritual died long ago, but the dollies survive as a country craft; they are still widely believed to bring 'good luck'. This craftsman is making a selection of pagan and Christian motifs including horseshoes and crosses.*

to delay the birth of her husband's mortal son: the delay allows a rival prince to be born first and thus to claim the throne over Herakles. What we would now term 'witchcraft' was originally Celtic pagan religious lore and ritual, suppressed by Christianity. The tying of complex magical knots has its counterpart in the interwoven forms of Celtic art. The repetitions originate in the oral tradition but also increase the ritual atmosphere of the piece.

The song was recorded by a pioneer in the English folk-song revival, Martin Carthy, who sings it to the tune of a traditional Breton drinking-song, Son ar Chistr (Song of Cider), which has itself been recorded by Alan Stivell. The tune was apparently composed in 1930 by a Breton piper who is now a Paris tramp. Such borrowings of tunes and changes of fortune must also have been present in the life and work of the ancient Celtic bards.

BELOW **Martin Carthy.** *The English solo singer and guitarist also performs with the Watersons, Dave Swarbrick, and John Kirkpatrick, all of them pioneers in the revival of English folk song and dance. His songs range from the collected folk material of the Celtic fairy and British historical past to the contemporary lyrics of Leon Rosselson, on subjects such as Britain's war with Argentina over the Falkland Islands.*

bells and ten,
'There's hanging fifty bells
  and ten.
'This goodly gift shall be your
  own,
'If back to my own truelove
  you'll turn again
'That she might bear her baby
  son.'

'O but child, she will never
  lighter be,
'Nor from sickness will she
  e'er be free;
'But she will die and she will
  turn to clay,
'And you will wed with
  another maid.'
And sighing, says this weary
  man,
As back to his own truelove
  he's gone again:
'I wish my life was at an end.'

King Willy back to his
  mother he did run
And he's gone there as a
  begging son.
He says: 'My truelove has this
  fine golden girdle,
'Set with jewels all about the
  middle.
'At every part of this girdle's
  hem
'There's hanging fifty bells
  and ten
'There's hanging fifty silver
  bells and ten,
'This goodly gift shall be your
  own,
'If back to my own truelove
  you'll turn again
'That she might bear her baby
  son.'

'Oh but child, she will never
  lighter be,
'Nor from sickness will she
  e'er be free;
'But she will die and she will
  turn to clay,
'And you will wed with
  another maid.'
And sighing, says this weary
  man,

123

As back to his own truelove
   he's gone again:
'I wish my life was at an end.'

Well up and spoke his noble
   queen;
And she has told King Willy
   of a plan
How she might bear her baby
   son.
She says: 'You must go, get
   you down to the market
   place,
'And you must buy you a loaf
   of wax;
'And you must shape it as a
   babe that is to nurse
'And you must make two eyes
   of glass.
'Ask your mother to the
   christening day,
'And you must stand there
   close as you can be,
'That you might hear what
   she do say."

King Willy, he's gone down
   to the market place,
and he has bought him a loaf
   of wax;
And he has shaped it as a
   babe that is to nurse,
And he has made two eyes of
   glass.
He asked his mother to the
   christening day,
And he has stood there close
   as he could be,
That he might hear what she
   did say.
And how she stormed and
   how she swore:
She's spied the babe where no
   babe could be before,
She's spied the babe where
   none could be before.

She says: 'Who was it undid
   the nine witch-knots,
'Braided in amongst this
   lady's locks?
'And who was it who took
   out the combs of care,
'Braided in amongst this
   lady's hair?

LEFT **Green Man: capital of door column of the Church of St Mary and St David, Kilpeck, near Hereford, England** *(twelfth century* AD*). The pagan fertility god was used to 'scare away the evil eye' in many medieval Christian churches. His staring eyes and the tendrils emerging from his mouth demonstrate the continuing stylistic traditions of Celtic art.*

'And who was it slew the
   master kid,
'That ran and slept all
   beneath this lady's bed,
'That ran and slept all
   beneath her bed?
'And who was it unlaced her
   left shoe?
'And who was it that let her
   lighter be,
'That she might bear her
   baby boy?'

And it was Willy who undid
   the nine witch-knots,
Braided in amongst this lady's
   locks.
And it was Willy who took
   out the combs of care,
Braided in amongst this lady's
   hair.
And it was Willy the master
   kid did slay,
And it was Willy who
   unlaced her left-foot shoe,
And he has let her lighter be.
And she has poured out a
   baby son,
And prayed to the blessings
   that be them upon,
And prayed to the blessings
   them upon.

FURTHER READING

MYTHS, LEGENDS AND FOLKTALES

Most of the following translations and versions are readily available in paperback:

Barber, R (ed), *The Arthurian Legends* (Woodbridge and Wolfeboro, 1979)
Beroul, *The Romance of Tristan* (trans. A S Fedrick; Harmondsworth, 1970)
A Celtic Miscellany (trans. K H Jackson; Harmondsworth, 1971)
Early Irish Myths and Sagas (trans. J Gantz; Harmondsworth, 1981)
Gottfried von Strassburg, *Tristan* (trans. A T Hatto; Harmondsworth, 1960)
The Mabinogion (trans. G Jones and T Jones; illustrated by Alan Lee; Hendrik-Ido-Ambacht, 1982)
The Mabinogion (trans. J Gantz; Harmondsworth, 1976)
Malory, *Le Morte d'Arthur* (Harmondsworth, 1969)
Rolleston, T W, *Myths and Legends of the Celtic Race* (London, 1985)
Scott, M, *Irish Folk and Fairy Tales Omnibus* (Harmondsworth, 1989)
The Tain (trans. T Kinsella; Dublin 1969 and London 1970)
Williamson, R, *The Craneskin Bag: Celtic Stories and Poems* (Edinburgh, 1989)
Wilson, B K, *Scottish Folk-Tales and Legends* (Oxford, 1954)

SUITABLE FOR YOUNGER READERS

Jacobs, J (ed), *Celtic Fairy Tales* (London, 1970)
Cooper, S, *The Dark is Rising Sequence* (London 1984)
Dickinson, P, *Merlin Dreams* (illustrated by Alan Lee; London, 1988)
Garner, A, *Elidor* (London, 1965); *The Weirdstone of Brisingamen* (London, 1960); *The Moon of Gomrath* (London, 1963); *The Owl Service* (London, 1967); *Red Shift* (London, 1973)

INTERPRETATION

The following modern studies of Celtic Mythology are also of interest:

Matthews, C, *Mabon and the Mysteries of Britain: An Exploration of the Mabinogion* (London, 1987)
Matthews, J & C, *The Aquarian Guide to British and Irish Mythology* (Wellingborough, 1988)
Rutherford, W, *Celtic Mythology* (Wellingborough, 1987)
Senior, M, *Myths of Britain* (London, 1979)

VARIANT SPELLINGS AND PRONUNCIATION GUIDE

Spellings of Celtic names are inconsistent from source to source. Anglicizations are generally attempts to reproduce the sound rather than the spelling of the words. Here is a selected list of characters and places with some of their variant spellings. Pronunciations are given only for major figures.

MYTHOLOGICAL GROUPS

(A) Arthurian; (I) Irish; (S) Scottish; (W) Welsh

Ailill ['ailitl] (I)
Albain/Albion/Britain
Allen (S) / Ainle (I)
Aod/Aed [id] (I)
Arden (S) / Ardan (I)
Bedwyr ['bedwir] (W) / Bedivere (A)
Bendigeidfran [bendi'gaydfran] / Bran the Blessed (W)
Branwen ['branoowen] (W)
Bricriu ['brikru] (I)
Brigit/Brigit/Bride (I) (S)
Caswallawn [kas'watloun] (W) / Cassivellaunos
Cathbad ['kafuv] (I)
Cei/Cai/Kay/Keu [kai] (A)
Conchobar mac Nessa ['konchovor] (I) / Connachar [conn'acher] (S)
Connla/Conle ['konlle] (I)
CuChulainn/Cú Chulaind [ku'chulinn] (I)
Culhwch ['kilhooch] (W)
Custennin [küs'tenhin] (W)
Dearg ['dayarg] (I)
Deirdriu ['derrdru] / Deirdre ['derrdri] (I)
Efnissien [ev'nissien] (W)
Erin/Ireland
Etain/Édaín ['edain] (I)
Ferchar ['ferchar] (S) / Fergus (I)
Fingula/Fionnuala
Gwalchmai [goo'alchmai] (W) / Gawain (A)
Gwrhyr ['goohrir] (W)
Harddlech/Harlech ['harthlech] (W)
Isolt/Iseult/Yseult/Isolde (A)
Llŷr [tleer] (W)
Manannan ['mannernan] (I)
Manawydan [man'ouithan] (W)
Matholwch [math'olooch] (W)
Medb/Medhbh/Maeve [methv] (I)
Naoisi/Naois ['noisi] (I)
Oifa/Aoife ['ifer] (I)
Ove/Aobh ['iver] (I)
Pryderi [pri'deri] (W)
Pwyll ['pooitl] (W)
Rhiannon [hri'annon] (W)
Sidhe [shee] (I)
Sualtam ['suerllterm] (I)
Twrch Trwyth [toorch'trooeeth] (W)
Uisnech/Usnach ['usnerch] (I)
Yspaddaden [usba'thaden] (W)

PRONUNCIATION KEY:

['] = before stressed syllable; [ch] = ch in Scottish 'loch'; [ou] = Welsh aw as ou in 'out'; [th] = Welsh dd as th in 'there'; [tl] = Welsh ll as tl in 'little'; [oo] = Welsh w as oo in 'cook'; Welsh u and y = i as in 'pill'; Stresses generally come on the penultimate syllable.

CELTIC CULTURE, SURVIVAL, AND INFLUENCE

Alcock, L, *Arthur's Britain* (Harmondsworth, 1971)

Bord, J & B, *A Guide to Ancient Sites in Britain* (London, 1979)

Ellis, P B, *Celtic Inheritance* (London, 1985)

Filip, J, *Celtic Civilization and its Heritage* (Prague, 1962)

Green, M, *The Gods of the Celts* (Gloucester and New Jersey 1986); *Symbol and Image in Celtic Religion* (London and New York, 1989)

Henderson, I, *The Picts* (London, 1967)

Ireland, S, *Roman Britain: A Sourcebook* (London and Sydney, 1986)

Laing, L, *Celtic Britain* (London, 1979); *Later Celtic Art in Britain and Ireland* (Aylesbury, 1987)

Lloyd, J, *A History of Wales* (London, 1939)

Megaw, R & V, *Art of the European Iron-Age* (London 1970); *Early Celtic Art in Britain and Ireland* (Aylesbury, 1986)

Nordenfalk, C, *Celtic and Anglo-Saxon Painting* (New York, 1977)

Piggott, S, *The Druids* (London, 1968)

Powell, T G E, *The Celts* (London, 1958)

Raftery, J (ed), *The Celts* (Cork, 1964)

Rees, A & B, *Celtic Heritage* (London, 1961)

Ritchie, W F & J N G, *Celtic Warriors* (Aylesbury, 1985)

Rodwell, W (ed), *Temples, Churches and Religion in Roman Britain* (British Archaeological Report 77, Oxford 1980)

Ross, A, *A Traveller's Guide to Celtic Britain* (London 1985); *The Pagan Celts* (London, 1986)

Ross, A and Robins, D, *The Life and Death of a Druid Prince* (London, 1989)

Sharkey, J, *Celtic Mysteries* (London, 1975)

CELTIC MYTHOLOGY AND FOLK-TALE IN MUSIC

The following are available on record and cassette:

Martin Carthy, *Crown of Horn* (Topic, 1976)

Planxty, *Words and Music* (WEA, 1983)

Henry Purcell, *King Arthur* (cond. John Eliot Gardiner; Erato)

Alan Stivell, *Legend* (Celtic Music, 1987)

Richard Wagner, *Tristan und Isolde* (various)

Robin Willimson, *Music for the Mabinogi* (Claddagh Records, 1983)

Index

Acknowledgements

The author would like to extend special thanks to Gwen for her hospitality, Tony for his archeology, Christina for her images, Joan for her Iseult, Planxty for their music, and Alan Lee for his paintings.

Picture Credits

The author and publishers would also like to thank the following for the use of picture material in this book:

Bath Museum: pages 10 (photo. Fotek), 11, *l*, 11 *r* (photo. Fotek). © **David Bellingham:** pages 16, 18, 28, 44 *b*, 46, 47, 57, 69, 77, 81 *b*, 101 *r*, 109, 112, 113, 117, 122 *t*, 124. **Birmingham Museum and Art Gallery:** pages 86, 90. **The Bodleian Library, Oxford:** page 84. **Musée Calvet, Avignon:** page 68. **City Art Centre, Edinburgh:** page 106. **Claddagh Records Ltd/photo. Janet Williamson:** page 49 *l*. **Commissioners of Public Works, Ireland:** page 42. **C M Dixon, Canterbury:** pages 7 *r*, 9 *l* (British Museum, London), 9 *r*, 17 (The Museum of Antiquities, Newcastle-upon-Tyne University), 19 *l* (Naturhist. Museum, Vienna), 20 (National Museum, Budapest), 21 (National Museum, Copenhagen), 23 *l* (National Museum, Copenhagen), 24 *t b* (National Museum, Copenhagen), 25, 26 *tl* (British Museum, London), 26 *bl r*, 27 (British Museum, London), 32 *l* (Cluny, Paris), 32 *r*, 33, 34, 35–6 (British Museum, London), 39, 41, 43 (Württemberg Landesmuseum, Stuttgart), 44 *t* (British Museum, London), 49 *r* (Victoria and Albert Museum, London), 52 (Prahistorische Staatsammlung, Munich), 53 *t* (The Museum of Antiquities, Newcastle-upon-Tyne University), 53 *b* (British Museum, London), 54 (British Museum, London), 55 (Netherhall Collection) 56, 59 *t* (Bucharest Museum, Romania), 59 *b* (Museum of Antiquities, Newcastle-upon-Tyne University), 60 (National Museum, Copenhagen), 61 (British Museum, London), 63, 65 (British Museum, London), 66 (Viking Ships Museum, Bygdøy, Oslo), 67 (National Museum, Copenhagen), 71 (National Museum of Antiquities, Bucharest), 78 *l* (National Museum, Copenhagen), 78 *r* (British Museum, London), 79 (National Museum, Copenhagen), 80, 82 (National Museum of Wales), 83 (National Museum of Ireland, Dublin), 92, 94 (National Museum, Budapest), 95 (Museum of National Antiquities, Stockholm), 96 *t* (Corbridge Museum, Northumberland), 96 *c*, 96 *b* (Musée Borely, Marseilles), 100 *l*, 103 (National Museum of Antiquities, Stockholm), 105 (British Museum, London), 108 (British Museum, London), 119 (National Museum of Antiquities, Edinburgh), 123. **Dundee Art Galleries and Museums:** pages 29, 45. **General Post Office, Dublin:** page 23 *r*. **Glasgow Art Gallery and Museum:** page 37. © **C Grande:** pages 102, 115, 120. **Hayling Island Excavation Project/photo. G Soffe:** page 72 *t*. **Humberside County Council Archeology Unit:** page 19 *r*. © **Tony King:** pages 7 *l*, 8 *r*, 72 *b*, 73 *t b*, 74–5, 110. **Lambeth Palace Library/MS 6, f.43 v,** © 1981 LPL/photo. Mike Gunn: page 107. © **Alan Lee:** pages 64, 81 *t*, 93. **Peter Nahum Ltd:** page 87. **The National Gallery of Ireland:** pages 12, 118. **The National Museum of Ireland:** page 111. **National Galleries of Scotland, Edinburgh:** pages 15, 38, 97. © **Quintet Publishing Ltd/photo. Trevor Wood:** pages 31, 51. **Skyscan Balloon Photography Copyright:** pages 6, 22, 62, 100 *r*. **Topic Records/photo. Dave Peabody:** page 122 *b*. **Trinity College Library, Dublin:** page 48. © **Sheree Wilson:** page 8 *l*.

Front jacket: Gundestrup Cauldron, Denmark (National Museum, Copenhagen).
Back jacket: Scorhill Bronze-Age stone circle, Dartmoor, England (David Bellingham).